Seashells

BY R. TUCKER ABBOTT

A Ridge Press Book

Bantam Books
Toronto • New York • London

Photo Credits

BC—Bruce Coleman
SL—Sea Library
TS—Tom Stack & Associates

R. Tucker Abbott: 20, 27, 34 (rt.), 38, 43, 45, 47 (top), 54 (btm.), 60, 61, 67, 79, 91, 92, 93, 97 (btm.), 100, 108, 110, 111, 112, 119 (top), 125, 142, 144, 148, 149; Alice Denison Barlow: 21, 24, 33, 35, 37, 39, 40, 41, 42, 48, 49 (btm.), 51, 54 (top), 58, 59, 64, 69, 71, 72, 73, 74, 76, 78, 83 (top), 87, 90, 96, 103 (top), 104, 115 (btm.), 120, 121 (rt.), 126, 127, 128, 131, 134, 137, 141, 145, 146 (btm.), 147, 150 (top & mid.), 152, 153, 154, 155 (top), 156 (btm.); Jen & Des Bartlett (BC): 86 (btm.); Jane Burton (BC): 47 (btm.), 133 (top); Don M. Byrne: 6 (top), 55, 89 (btm.), 95, 116 (btm.); James H. Carmichael, Jr. (BC): 3, 4, 5, 49 (top), 52 (top), 68-69, 80, 89 (top), 116 (top), 122, 150 (btm.), 151; Henry Chaney: 106 (btm.); Neville Coleman (SL): 6 (btm.), 22, 85, 129, 156 (top); Ellen Crovo: 9, 97 (top); Jeff Foott: 13; Neville Fox-Davies (BC): 132; Keith Gillett (TS): 109 (btm.); Warren Krupsaw: 26, 29, 66, 75, 138; Nina Leen: 28, 52 (btm.), 106 (top), 140, 146 (top); Hal Lewis: 77; Robert Lipe: 57 (btm.), 83 (btm.), 84 (top), 107, 133 (btm.); D. Lyons (BC): 31, 32, 34 (left), 56 (rt.), 155 (btm.); Virginia Maes: 124; Marine Studios, Marineland, St. Augustine: 62; Max Marrow: 70, 103 (btm.); Giuseppe Mazza: 27 (btm.), 30, 46, 50, 56 (left), 63, 82, 86 (top), 94, 99 (btm.), 101, 109 (top), 113, 115 (top), 121 (left), 136, 143; David K. Mulliner: 105; David Namias: 36, 44, 53, 65, 114, 117, 119 (btm.); D. M. Opresko: 135; George Raeihle: 57 (top); J. Rosewater: 123; Sacha (SL): 23; Nicholas J. Saia: 139; Roger & Joy Spurr (BC): 130; W. M. Stephens (TS): 99 (top); Ron Taylor (SL): 25; Ronald F. Thomas (BC): 81, 84 (btm.); Barry R. Wilson: 98

Front Cover: Regal Murex and Harp Shell, David Namias
Back Cover: White-spotted Margin Shell, Robert Lipe
Title Page: Top left, Camel Cowrie, Giuseppe Mazza; bottom left, Painted Top Shell, Jane Burton (BC); right, Cerith, Giuseppe Mazza
Maps: Tony Pannoni

SEASHELLS
*A Bantam Book/published by arrangement with
The Ridge Press, Inc.*

PRINTING HISTORY
*Bantam edition published February 1976
2nd printing . . . . August 1978*

ISBN 0-553-12318-1

Library of Congress Catalog Card Number: 75-21602

Published simultaneously in the United States and Canada

*Bantam Books are published by Bantam Books, Inc. Its trade-
mark, consisting of the words "Bantam Books" and the por-
trayal of a bantam, is registered in the United States Patent
Office and in other countries. Marca Registrada. Bantam
Books, Inc., 666 Fifth Avenue, New York, New York 10019.*

PRINTED IN ITALY BY MONDADORI EDITORE, VERONA

9 8 7 6 5 4 3 2

Contents

Cowries

Cone shells

Augers

▲Sieve Cowrie ▼Paper Nautilus

Introduction

Why Study Shells?

Few studies associated with nature and, in particular, with the oceans around us have intrigued more people than conchology, the study of shells. Not only are there legions of shell collectors in many parts of the world, but there are many scientists and shellfishing experts who devote their lives to investigating the biology and habits of these beautiful and useful creatures.

The appeal of conchology lies in the many-faceted nature of the hobby—it may take one into the field to enjoy the seashore; offer a chance to examine the curious habits of the mollusks that make shells; open the door to man's historical interest in shells in art and religion; and give the satisfaction of building an educational collection.

Edible mollusks, such as clams, oysters, and scallops, serve as a major source of protein for many millions of people, and, as advances are made in the science of mariculture, they will become increasingly important in a world that is becoming more and more polluted. New anti-viral and anti-cancer substances have recently been discovered in certain sea snails and marine clams. Medical investigators are equally interested in discovering how to control certain tropical fresh-water snails that carry parasitic diseases fatal to man.

For the lovers of beauty, shells have always offered a wide variety of opportunities for man to express himself, in the carving of exquisite cameos and in the creation of shell mosaics and shellcraft découpages. Precious pearls from oysters and objects carved from mother-of-pearl have been treasured since earliest times.

Not only can the study of shells enlighten the student in the ways of nature but it can lead to new methods in anti-pollution work and programs of conservation. Even the lowly mollusk serves in the vital food chains of life and in the natural ways of recycling the elements of living creatures.

Mollusks—the Makers of Shells

Seashells are familiar objects, but the fact that they are the outer, shelly homes of living, soft-bodied creatures is not generally known. Shells are made by many kinds of living forms—an egg shell by birds, a coconut shell by a palm tree, a tortoise shell by an aquatic turtle, and a barnacle shell by a member of the crab clan. Seashells are made by mollusks, a unique group or phylum of sea creatures known familiarly to most of us as clams, oysters, scallops, conchs, periwinkles, and whelks. The sea urchin and sand dollar, although they may resemble molluscan seashells, are members of the starfish phylum and are not mollusks.

Mollusks, which curiously also include the squids and the octopus, are soft-bodied, backboneless creatures having two unique organs not found in any other invertebrates. One of these is the mantle, a fleshy, cape-like organ that surrounds the mantle cavity where the gills, anus, kidney exits, and smell organs are located. The mantle is unique in having many microscopic glands that produce the shell of a clam or snail. The second unique organ, present in all mollusks except clams, is the radula. This is a long, tongue-like organ, bearing many sharp, hook-like teeth. The radula is used to rasp and lick at food somewhat in the manner of a cat's tongue lapping up milk.

Not all mollusks produce shells, although they will have the typical molluscan features, such as a mantle and a radula. Examples of shell-less mollusks are the octopus, most squids, garden slugs, and nudibranch marine snails. The largest known living mollusk is a 73-foot giant squid of New Zealand that has no shell. The largest shelled mollusk is the giant *Tridacna* clam of the southwest Pacific. Adults grow to a length of about 4½ feet, and the two valves and internal soft parts may have a combined weight of 500 pounds. In contrast, the smallest adult clams and snails may have a maximum length of 1.0mm, which is half the size of a grain of rice!

Mollusks are the second-largest group in the animal kingdom, exceeded only by the insects in numbers of different kinds. There are about 60,000 known living species and, of course, many more extinct fossil species. Mollusks are found in almost every corner of the world. There are numerous kinds that live on land—in the gardens, woods, tropical rain forests, high in trees, on the slopes of the highest mountains, and under bushes in the driest of deserts. Fresh-water snails and pearly mussels are found in the ponds, lakes, streams, and major rivers of the world.

Lima File Clam

Marine shells are found in all the seas of the world, and they have chosen almost every possible living place from the rocky shores high above the tide marks to the deepest parts of the ocean. Some live safely buried in sand, while others have taken on a life of burrowing into hard clay, coral, or wood. There are parasitic mollusks that live attached to other sea creatures, such as the holothurian sea puddings, the starfish, and the alcyonarian seafans and seawhips.

Mollusks are an important and vital part of the ecology and economy of the sea. Not only do they serve as the main source of food for many economically important food fishes such as the cod, halibut, and floun-der, but some families of mollusks, such as the oyster, clam, and scallop, are a major source of protein for humans. From the pearl oyster come pearls and mother-of-pearl shell materials. Some shells, like the strange shipworm clam, *Teredo*, are known as the most destructive bivalves in the ocean and account for millions of dollars in losses to wooden boats, wharf pilings, and marine rope.

Shell Classes

The great clan of molluscan seashells belongs to a group, or phylum, of the animal kingdom known as the Mollusca. The word comes from the Latin, *mollis*, meaning soft. This might seem to be a contradiction, since hard seashells are anything but soft; but the word Mollusca was first coined by the early Greek philosopher, Aristotle, who was referring to the soft octopus, the squid, and to the snail-like *Aplysia* sea hares. Other sea creatures, like the tritons, oysters, and clams, have soft bodies, but **9** they produce hard external shells.

During the evolutionary development of the mollusks, through many millions of years, there have evolved seven main types which are, for the sake of convenience, recognized as classes. Each class, such as the Bivalvia (clams, oysters, scallops, etc.), has a very distinctive set of characteristics that sets it off from the other major classes.

Class **Gastropoda:** The gastropods, or univalves, include about 30,000 kinds of snails, whelks, limpets, and slugs, and are characterized by having a distinct head, bearing tentacles and eyes, and in having a creeping foot. Most species produce a single, coiled shell, and most have a set of radular teeth. Snail univalves are found in marine, brackish, fresh-water, and terrestrial habitats.

These univalves are divided into three quite different groups or subclasses: the **Prosobranchia** ("fore-gilled" snails) which include the majority of the snails included in this book, such as the abalones, periwinkles, whelks, volutes, cones, etc. They have a mantle cavity containing a set of gills, and most species have an operculum. The subclass **Pulmonata** includes the lung-bearing land snails that live in terrestrial habitats. Members of the marine subclass **Opisthobranchia** ("hind-gills") include the sea hares, bubble snails, and shell-less nudibranchs. The gills are generally posterior to the heart. Male and female organs are found in each individual in the last two subclasses.

Class **Bivalvia:** Characterized by the presence of two, interlocking, shelly valves and a hatchet-shaped foot, this class contains about 10,000 kinds of clams, mussels, cockles, and various oysters. They lack a head and have no radular teeth. Fresh-water mussels are common in ponds and rivers and have a mother-of-pearl interior surface. Some bivalves, such as the scallops, are capable of swimming by quickly snapping together their valves. Other clams are modified into wormshaped creatures that live in self-made burrows in wood, clay, and rock. Oysters and mussels either cement themselves or attach themselves by means of a thread-like byssus to wharves and rocks.

Class **Cephalopoda:** The Chambered Nautilus, squids, and the octopus make up this class of active mollusks. They have eight or more arms bearing many circular suckers. A radula and a parrot-like beak are present in most of the 400 species, all of which live in the sea.

Four other minor classes live exclusively in the sea: the class **Polyplacophora** contains about 500 kinds of chitons, snail-like creatures with eight shell plates held together by a leathery border, or girdle.

Members of the rare class **Aplacophora** are worm-like and are covered by microscopic scales. They live in deep water. The class **Scaphopoda** contains about 300 kinds of tusk shells which are open at each end and rarely exceed a length of 4 inches. They live buried in sand in deep water, and feed by means of numerous filament-like tentacles. Rarest of the classes is the **Monoplacophora,** a group of strange, limpet-like mollusks that have some parts of their bodies, such as the gills and kidneys, duplicated in segments similar to those in worms. These gastoverms are known from only a few species because they live at very great depths in the sea. All of the minor classes have a typical molluscan radula.

How Shapes and Colors Are Made

Mollusks, like all other forms of life on our planet, produce young very similar to themselves, mainly through the inheritance of genetic characters. A Pink Conch of the Bahamas will produce long, gelatinous egg strands which will hatch within a few weeks and grow into small, then large, Pink Conchs. The shape of a shell is produced by the shelly material, or calcium carbonate, that the fleshy mantle exudes.

Some snails look quite different as young specimens. As they continue to grow by adding more shell material to the outer lip, they will finally produce a greatly thickened and expanded outer lip. Thus, the broad, flaring lip of the Pink Conch or the Fighting Conch is a sign of maturity. Cowries start out as simple, thin-lipped shells resembling olive shells in shape, but once they grow to maturity, the outer lips are thickened up, beset with shelly teeth, and curled inwards by additional growth. The spines and ribs of murex shells are produced by folds and protuberances in the edge of the mantle.

Many snails and clams take from three to five years to reach maturity and then may continue to live for another ten years. However, some forms, such as the scallops, have a life span of only two or three years. The huge, 500-pound giant clams of the Pacific are believed to be upwards of 75 years old.

Coloration in the shell material comes from pigments produced by special glands embedded in the edge of the mantle. Bands, zigzag lines, and triangles are produced by the migration and sporadic production of pigments by these special glands. The diet of a mollusk can have an effect on the extent of coloration. Rarely, a pigmentless "albino" shell may be produced by accident of birth.

How Mollusks Feed

Mollusks demonstrate almost every variation possible in their search for nutrients, and the feeding habits of seashells vary from that of docile herbivores to rapacious carnivores. Some snails like the wentletraps are external parasites on sea anemones, while other curious, shell-less snails live inside holothurian sea puddings, sucking up the body fluids of their hosts.

Most mollusks, with the exception of all bivalves, feed by means of a strong set of radular teeth. This belt of hooked teeth is rasped back and forth, not only to tear away plant material or flesh, but, in some carnivorous snails, to bore holes in sea urchins and other seashells. Herbivores, such as the *Strombus* conchs, the periwinkles, and many freshwater snails, feed steadily on aquatic plants and algae. The California sea hare is capable of eating over five pounds of seaweed a day. A set of hard gizzard stones, located in the stomach, grinds up the weed. Other herbivores, including most kinds of bivalves and a few snails, such as the *Crepidula* slipper shells, filter fine, planktonic algae from the ocean water.

While most chitons are herbivorous, one species in California captures and feeds upon live shrimp by raising up its front end and snapping it down quickly on its victim. Squid are probably the most active of the carnivores. They stalk schools of small fish and then suddenly dart in, grasp a fish with the tentacles, and bite a large chunk of flesh from the neck of the fish. Octopi feed on crabs and other mollusks, usually dragging their victims into their lairs. Strangest of the carnivores are the fish-spearing cone snails of the southwest Pacific. Small goby fish are harpooned by a long, needle-like radular tooth, injected with a fatal venom, and then slowly swallowed whole.

How Mollusks Reproduce

In most marine mollusks the sexes are separate, with the task of egg production and, in some cases, egg protection being done by the female. In most of the bivalves and in some of the primitive snails, such as the limpets and top shells, the microscopic eggs are shed freely into the water. At the same time, the nearby males give off millions of sperm, so that fertilization takes place in the ocean water. Among the higher snails, such as the conchs and whelks, fertilization is accomplished by copulation, and in most cases the female produces a clump of horny capsules into which the eggs are placed.

Tide pools, Pacific coast

A few bivalves, such as the scallops, all land snails, and the opisthobranch sea snails and bubble shells, are bisexual, with both male and female organs in each individual. Some mollusks, such as the oyster and the slipper shells, change from males to females during the last part of their lives.

Egg capsules of snails may be in the shape of jelly-like mounds, long spaghetti strands, or may be horny and shaped like drinking glasses, urns, or thick coins. The octopus and squid lay jelly-like festoons of eggs under rock ledges, and the female protects them until the young hatch.

Once an egg becomes fertilized, it soon develops into a larval form known as the trochophore, and finally, in some cases, changes to a free-swimming veliger with tiny cilia to assist it in maneuvering. Within a few days or weeks the veliger will produce a shell and then sink to the bottom of the ocean to begin a normal life. In some families the young develop within the egg capsule and emerge as crawling snails. There are some snails that brood their young in the mantle cavity or the oviduct and give birth to live young.

Shell Names

Knowing the correct name of a shell makes it possible to consult scientific literature for additional information about the habits, biology, and distribution of the species. It also permits the collector to place the species in its proper place in a collection well organized according to family and class relationships. While collecting in the ocean, it is not necessary to know the name of a shell, but once you clean it, put it in the collection, and attempt to exchange extra specimens with other collectors, the proper name will become important.

Common or vernacular names are not very satisfactory or accurate because different parts of the same country may use the same name for different shells—a conch in New Hampshire is a *Busycon,* in Florida it is a *Strombus* or *Pleuroploca.* And, of course, the French, Japanese, and Italians have entirely different shell names. For this reason, a system of **13** two Latin names is used to name each species. This binomial system, started officially in 1758, is universally accepted. Latin names are not always difficult—we use them daily, such as gorilla, chrysanthemum, patella, and zebra. The two names given to shells are akin to "John Jones," except that they are reversed, thus "Jones john." In shells it would be *Conus* (the genus name) and *albus* (the species name). Note that the species name is never capitalized and that scientific names are printed in *italics*. After the species name is placed the name of the scientist who first described and named the species: *Conus albus* Smith.

In order to place each species in its proper scheme of classification, a series of higher groupings are used to show relationships. In other words, there may be several species in one genus. But if there are several genera that are closely related, they are placed in a family, such as Conidae (not italicized). Families are grouped together in Orders, and so forth. An example of a detailed classification would be:

Classification	Other examples
Phylum: Mollusca (Mollusks)	Echinodermata (starfish, etc.)
Class: Gastropoda (Snails)	Bivalvia (Clams)
Superfamily: Strombacea (Conchs)	Naticacea (Moon Snails)
Family: Strombidae (Conchs)	Aporrhaidae (Pelican's Foot)
Genus: *Strombus* (True Conchs)	*Lambis* (Spider Conchs)
Species: *gigas* Linné (Queen Conch)	*costatus* Gmelin (Milk Conch)

Where to Look for Shells

The seashore, the reefs, and the shallow, sandy bays have their seasons and changing moods. These varying conditions combined with the reproductive cycles of the mollusks cause shell populations to wax and wane. However, there are certain places that various kinds of mollusks prefer to inhabit. If you know something of the habits and preferences of mollusks, you are more likely to discover their hiding places.

The seabeach is generally inhospitable to most mollusks, except for bivalves like the coquinas or wedge clams that can rapidly burrow back into the sand. Hot sun, cold air temperatures, shifting sands, and pounding surf are not tolerated by shy mollusks. Some beaches, however, become heavily laden with stranded shells after severe off-land storms.

The beaches of west Florida, South Africa, and the windward side of tropical islands are likely to be heavily strewn with freshly killed mollusk shells during the windiest seasons.

Intertidal zones are readily accessible areas for the collector, whether they be the tidepools of gently sloping rocky shores or the vast sandy or muddy flats of shelter lagoons or bays. In northern areas along the rocky coasts, pools left by the receding tide shelter a host of interesting periwinkles, dogwinkles, and limpets. Most of these are hidden under festoons of seaweeds or among clumps of the Blue Mussel. On sand flats, small holes made by the siphons of bivalves and winding trails left by snails will reveal the presence of mollusks.

Most live shells are found from the low-tide mark to a depth of about 100 feet. During the day most mollusks hide in the sand, among algae, or in the crevices of rocks. Many species live and lay eggs under slabs of dead coral. Snorkeling, scuba-diving, and using a small mesh hand sieve or dredge are all effective in locating specimens. Collecting at night with a light is usually productive.

Clams and snails may be cleaned by boiling them for ten minutes and then pulling out the soft parts with a pin or hook. Freezing for several days is also effective.

Ocean Provinces of the World

Each major part of the world has a unique ocean with its own special temperatures and water-current conditions. The plants and animals of these oceans are for the most part quite different from those of neighboring seas, although there are many species, particularly the pelagic ones of the open seas, that are worldwide in distribution. There are five tropical and about 12 cold-water provinces of the world. Only the major ones are outlined here.

The **Indo-Pacific Province** is the largest and warmest of the world seas; it stretches from the eastern shores of Africa over to India, the East Indies, to northern Australia, westward to Hawaii and eastern Polynesia. Cowries, cones, miters, volutes, olives, spider conchs, and giant clams abound in this province. The limits of the province are marked by the presence of coral reefs.

The **Caribbean Province** is the second largest in area, but has a comparatively poor representation of marine shells. Its area extends from central Brazil northward into the West Indies, southern Florida, and Bermuda. Helmet shells, tellins, *Strombus* conchs, a few cowries, and a couple of dozen kinds of cones are characteristic of its shell fauna

Scandinavia

ICELAND
GREAT BRITAIN

EUROPE

ASIA

AFRICA

INDIA

Cape
Verde
Islands

ANGOLA

Indian Ocean

South Atlantic Ocean

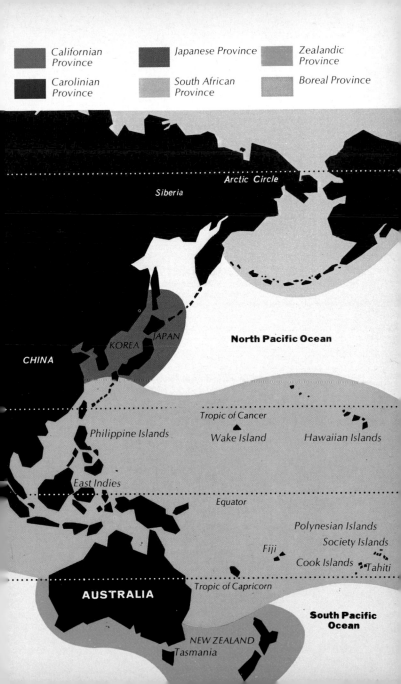

of about 1,500 species.

The **Panamanian Province,** despite its relatively small extent, is perhaps one of the richest in number of individuals as well as different species. This province is tropical in nature with its center on the Pacific side of Central America, but many of its shell members are found northward to Baja California and southward to Ecuador. Murex shells, dove shells, venus clams, and olives thrive in this province.

The tropical **West African Province** is small and confined to the western bulge of Africa from the Cape Verde Islands south to Angola. It is characterized by many bizarre kinds of margin shells, volutes, and strange giant cockles.

The **Mediterranean Province** is a formerly tropical sea that has been turning into a colder, temperate zone for the last few million years. Its colorful shell fauna is a mixture of tropical tritons and temperate scallops, dove shells, and rock shells. Its fauna extends into the Atlantic around southern France and around the northwest corner of Africa.

The **Arctic Province** surrounds the north polar regions and includes northern Canada, Greenland, and Siberia. There are few species in this region and all are dull in color.

North America is flanked by two major, temperate provinces. In the west is the **Californian Province,** running from Oregon to Baja California. Limpets, abalones, and dogwinkles abound along the shores of this rich, cool-water area. In the east, the **Carolinian Province** is a unique and relatively rich area characterized by bay scallops, quahog clams, and *Busycon* whelks. The area extends from about Virginia south to Texas.

Other important and distinctive provinces exist in various parts of the world. Richest of these is the **Japanese Province,** largely limited to the Japan-Korea area. Rare slit-shells, *Thatcheria* turrids, and strange star-shells are common to this region. Equally unique is the **South African Province,** where cold waters and rough seas are a haven for numerous large, beautiful limpets, the rare Fulton's Cowrie, the largest known margin shell, and colorful cold-water cones. The **Zealandic Province,** also a cold-water area, extends across southern Australia, Tasmania, and New Zealand. It has several large kinds of abalones, numerous limpets, and some strange cowries. The **Boreal Province** of the North Atlantic has many unique periwinkles, limpets, top shells, and mussels which abound not only in the British Isles and Scandinavia, but also in Iceland, Newfoundland, and northern New England. **19**

Adanson's Slit Shell

Perotrochus adansonianus Crosse & Fischer

The long slit in the side of the shell is the mark of a primitive family of deep-sea snails known as the pleurotomarians or emperor tops. Adanson's Slit Shell, reaching a length of about 7 inches, is found at depths of more than 400 meters off Bermuda and the islands of the Caribbean.

The slit shells are vegetarians, and have two internal gill feathers, one on each side of the slit. Of the 11 known living species, six occur in the Atlantic, one off South Africa, and four in the Indo-Pacific region. The family has existed since the Cambrian Period, some 500,000,000 years ago.

Ridged Abalone

Haliotis scalaris Leach

Known in America as abalones and in Europe as ormers, or sea ears, these strange-looking snail shells resemble the valves of a bivalve. Closer inspection reveals a coiled apex at one end, and a series of four to six holes in the shell through which water is expelled from the gill chamber. Abalones cling to subtidal rocks and at night browse on particular kinds of algae.

The Pacific coast of the United States has the largest and most abundant kinds in the world, although the Ridged Abalone, shown here, which reaches a length of 4 inches, is fairly common in South Australia.

The foot of the abalone makes a delicious seafood, not unlike the muscle of the scallop. The iridescent shell material is used extensively in the shellcraft industry. Misshapen, baroque pearls are sometimes found in the flesh of the abalone snail.

Donkey Ear Abalone

Haliotis asinina Linné

Although the shell of this common southwest Pacific abalone is only 2 or 3 inches in length, the soft animal parts are about twice as large. When attacked by a crab, octopus, or starfish, this abalone crawls away with remarkable speed. It lives in shallow water near coral reefs and feeds on algae. Like other abalones, the sexes are separate, and both sperm and eggs are shed freely into the water.

In the western United States the industry of abalone fishing is being jeopardized by a superabundance of sea otters, which regularly include the abalone in their diet. Elsewhere, restraints have been passed into law in order to prevent overfishing by shellfishery operators.

Except for two very small, deep-sea species, the genus is absent in the western Atlantic.

Great Keyhole Limpet
Megathura crenulata Sowerby

Although the shells of the family of keyhole limpets resemble those of the cap-shaped true limpets, they differ in having a venthole resembling a keyhole in the apex of the shell. This enables the animal to expel waste products without clogging the two feathery gills located in the mantle cavity near the head.

The black-mottled flesh of the 5-inch-long Great Keyhole Limpet is twice the size of the shell and partially covers it. This edible species is moderately common in the low-tide zone from central California to Baja California.

Similar species, some with higher outlines and resembling the shape of miniature volcanos, are common on rocky coasts in warm waters throughout the world. **23**

Spiked Limpet

Patella longicosta Lamarck

Limpets are highly adapted for life at the edge of the sea along rocky coasts where powerful waves pound against their shells. Their low, convex contours offer a minimum of resistance, and the uncoiled, cap-shaped shell permits the maximum development of a muscular foot. Limpets browse on fine algal growths and prefer to be active at low tide and during the dark hours. Some species travel several feet during the night and are capable of homing back to their original site by morning.

The Spiked Limpet, 3 inches across, is a common South African species. Limpets are worldwide in distribution, and some are used as food.

Commercial Top Shell

Trochus niloticus Linné

Members of the family of tropical trochids are characterized by their inverted-top shape, by a hard shell made of iridescent mother-of-pearl, and by a circular horny operculum, or trapdoor, of flexible brown material.

Among the largest of the trochids is the 6-inch Commercial Top Shell whose flesh is edible and whose shell is used in the manufacture of pearly buttons. The snail is a vegetarian and lives on algae-strewn ocean bottoms at a depth of 20 to 40 feet. The most extensive fisheries are in the Palau Islands, Micronesia, and in the Andaman Sea near India.

Sun Shell

Astraea heliotropium Martyn

The magnificent Sun Shell found in waters off the coast of New Zealand was first brought back to Europe by Captain James Cook in 1775. The originally discovered specimen, still preserved in Cambridge, England, bears a label reading "from Cloudy Bay, Cooks Straits, New Zealand." Unknown in Europe till Cook's second return, this is a capital specimen, and the more so for having the operculum (a shelly trapdoor) naturally fixed (to it). Today this species, 3 inches in diameter, is moderately common in waters 30 to 80 feet deep. Cook's specimen was probably brought up in mud attached to the ship's anchor.

The Sun Shell is characterized by numerous large, fluted scales, or spines, placed around the edge of the shell. Whenever the outer gray surface of the shell is worn away, the silvery, iridescent internal shell is revealed. Members of this group of snails are vegetarians.

▲ Carved shell

Green Turban
Turbo marmoratus Linné

For many centuries the 8-inch Green Turban has been a major source of high-grade mother-of-pearl. Chinese craftsmen were the first to use the thick, heavy shell for carving intricate figures and designs. There was a ready supply of the abundant sea snail throughout southeast Asia. In its natural state, the outer shell is a deep blue-green, but when polished it reflects a pearly-white iridescence.

The Green Turban has a huge circular operculum which may weigh as much as a pound. The snail lives in murky waters about 20 to 40 feet in depth and feeds exclusively on seaweeds. The sexes are separate and both eggs and sperm are shed freely into the water. An adult may take six years to reach a size of 7 or 8 inches.

Tapestry Turban

Turbo petholatus Linné

The Tapestry Turban, which rarely exceeds 3 inches, is probably the most attractive of the tropical turbans, for no two specimens sport exactly the same design and coloration. The exterior of the shell has a naturally smooth finish, and the interior is a rich mother-of-pearl. The shelly operculum which completely seals the opening of the shell has long been a favorite article of jewelry because of its sea-green, glossy finish.

The snail is abundant in many parts of the southwest Pacific and as far north as southern Japan. It lives on the outer edge of coral reefs where the ocean waters have a high content of dissolved oxygen.

Most turbans are edible and make a delicious, though not attractive-looking, shellfish stew.

Delphinula Shell
Angaria delphinus Linné

A native of the tropical Indo-Pacific from Africa to the South Sea Islands, the Delphinula Shell displays a great variation in the production of spines from one locality to another. Evidently, diet and local water conditions are responsible. In quiet waters, such as in old sunken shipwrecks or in protected sea caves, the snail produces very long, curved, delicate spines; but in shallow waters, where wave action is strong, the spines are very short, blunt, and much more numerous.

Experiments on other members of the family have shown that an abrupt change in the kind of seaweeds in the diet will produce a major change in the color of newly secreted shell. The operculum of the 3-inch Delphinula Shell is horny, brown, and circular. **29**

Pheasant Shell

Phasianella australis Gmelin

Although most members of this family are less than ¼ inch in size, the Pheasant Shell from South Australia is a relative giant, reaching a length of 2 inches. The species is characterized by an oval, white, shelly operculum, and a rather thin but very strong shell. Unlike that in other trochacean snails, the shell material lacks mother-of-pearl. The variations in color and design are almost infinite.

Being vegetarians, they are found abundantly in cool water among kelp beds. The foot of the snail bears long filaments which serve as feelers. The sexes are separate and the eggs shed freely into the water.

There are fewer than three dozen living members of the family **30** throughout the world.

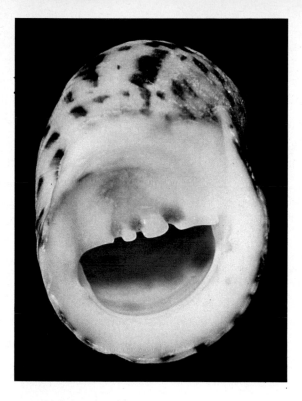

Bleeding Tooth

Nerita peloronta Linné

This common, inch-long snail of the Caribbean rocky shores is familiar to most shell collectors because of the peculiar blood-red stains around the white teeth in the aperture of the shell. This intertidal species browses on microscopic algae during the evening hours. Females lay tiny, dome-shaped, leathery capsules containing dozens of minute eggs. The young hatch out in several weeks and float to new areas.

Adults protect themselves from rock crabs and birds by means of a strong, shelly operculum which bears a shelly hook characteristic of most members of the neritid family.

Some species of neritids live in brackish water, others in fresh-water streams, and a few climb mangrove trees.

Pagoda Periwinkle

Tectarius coronatus Valenciennes

The largest member of the well-known family of littorinid snails is the Pagoda Periwinkle from the southwest Pacific. This rock-dweller lives just above the tidal zone where it can be alternately washed by sea spray and occasional rains. It sometimes reaches a length of 2 inches, although most of the many dozens of other species in the family rarely exceed a size of 1 inch.

Some periwinkles shed single egg capsules into the water, which then carries them to distant shores. A few species lay gelatinous egg masses, while others brood hundreds of shelled young in the oviduct of the female.

Periwinkles have a thin, oval operculum. They feed on detritus and algae with a toothed radular ribbon that is proportionately one of the longest found in any family of gill-bearing snails. Periwinkles are edible and are sold in the markets of Europe.

Sundial

Architectonica perspectivum Linné

The relatively uncommon sundials are mainly tropical, shallow-water dwellers, usually occurring in sandy areas. The Pacific Sundial reaches a diameter of about 2 inches and is characterized by a flat, many-whorled top and by a deep, round umbilicus on the underside. Into this depression fits the curious peg-like, chitinous operculum when the foot is extended and the animal crawling. Sometimes, recently hatched young snails take refuge in the umbilicus.

The food of the sundials may be the sessile marine animal called the sea pansy, since the snails are often found associated with this invertebrate. Some colorless sundials with very angulate, sharp-edged shells are found at depths of over 1,000 fathoms. Others are associated with colonies of soft corals.

32

Sundials ▶

Adult shells ▶
▼ Immature

Worm Shell

Vermicularia knorri Deshayes

Because their shells are very slender and long, members of the turritellid family have difficulty in moving about. Some species habitually remain buried in mud or sand and keep only the aperture just above the surface of the bottom. Others, like the worm shells, entwine themselves as they grow in corals or sponges or amongst clumps of other worm shells. In this sedentary state they must capture food by creating currents into the mantle cavity and over the sticky gills. The snout of the snail then engulfs the tiny food particles.

Knorr's Worm Shell, from the eastern United States, is coiled in a regular tight fashion for the first dozen turns but then grows in a very **34** loose, detached coil that sometimes reaches a length of 6 inches.

Turritella Snail
Turritella terebra Linné

These slender, mud-dwelling snails grow to a length of about 6 inches and are commonly found in the shallow waters of the Philippines and Indonesia. They are detritus-feeders preferring vegetable matter. The operculum is circular, very thin, and chitinous, with many whorls. Some species of turritellas lay stalked egg-capsules, while others brood their young within the oviduct. Fossil specimens many millions of years old have been found with numerous young shells inside the mother's shell.

There are over a hundred kinds of turritellas, and in some areas they are numerous enough to be gathered into great piles and burned to produce lime for masonry work.

Scaled Worm-shell

Serpulorbis squamigerus Carpenter

Most snails spend their lives crawling about in search of food and mates, but all members of the family of vermetid snails cement themselves to rocks, dead corals, or the upper surfaces of other kinds of large shells. Feeding is accomplished during the night by the snail's spinning long strands of mucus into the water immediately surrounding the area of the aperture. When the slime strands become covered with particles of floating food, they are pulled into the mouth of the snail one by one.

Some vermetid species grow in flat coils about 3 inches in diameter, such as the Scaled Worm-shell from western Central America, but a West Indian species is no larger than ⅛ inch and is very numerous on intertidal rocky shores.

Telescope Shell

Telescopium telescopium Linné

A large worldwide family of tropical snails lives in brackish intertidal areas near mangrove trees. They occur in enormous numbers on the surface of the black mudflats. Largest and heaviest is the handsome Telescope Shell of southeast Asia and the East Indies that grows to a length of 6 inches. They prefer the upper areas of the mudflats where the water reaches only at high tide and where the shade is heavy from the mangrove trees. They are foragers in algae-rich mud and generally feed only at night or during rainy periods.

Several kinds of smaller horn shells occur abundantly in Africa and the Caribbean, usually in brackish water areas.

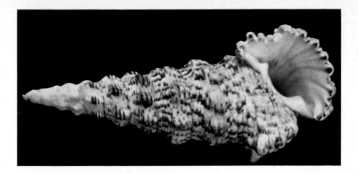

Giant Knobbed Cerith

Cerithium nodulosum Bruguière

Usually living in pure oceanic waters associated with sand and green algae, the cerith snails are among the most common and ubiquitous of snail shells. Few of the hundred or so kinds are colorful or attractive in design, but they serve as an important source of food for shallow-water, tropical fish and a few wading birds.

Largest of the living species is the Giant Knobbed Cerith from the Indo-Pacific area, which reaches a length of 4 or 5 inches. The largest known cerith from the Miocene fossil beds of Europe reached a length of 2 feet.

Some Caribbean species carry and spread a parasitic worm that affects birds but is harmless to man.

Precious Wentletrap

Epitonium scalare Linné

A longtime favorite of shell collectors, the Precious Wentletrap of the southwest Pacific was once greatly sought after, and during the nineteenth century commanded high prices at public shell auctions. It is reported that Asian craftsmen made counterfeit specimens from rice paste. Today, the shell is well known and its habitat in the Philippines and Australia sufficiently accessible, so that good, 2-inch-long specimens are available for a few dollars.

There are several hundred species in this family throughout the world. Most are white and may bear variously shaped ribs. Some feed on sea anemones; the eggs are laid in sand-covered strands.

39

◄ Precious Wentletraps

Onyx Slipper Shell

Crepidula onyx Sowerby

Slipper shells occur throughout temperate and tropical seas in shallow water where they attach themselves to other shells or pile up one upon the other. The shells are characterized by a flattish, shelly shelf or "poop-deck" inside the slipper or boat-shaped shell. No members of the family possess an operculum. They are planktonic feeders that filter out food by means of their curtain-like gills. Eggs are laid in capsules and brooded under the foot or in the mantle cavity.

The inch-long Onyx Slipper Shell from the Pacific side of Central America is one of a dozen common species, most of which are edible. The similar Common Atlantic Slipper Shell was introduced to Europe and is a nuisance on oyster beds.

Imbricate Cup-and-Saucer

Crucibulum spinosum Sowerby

The interesting architecture of this cup-shaped shell reminds one of a small cup sitting in a saucer. The cup is a shelly wall that reinforces the internal soft anatomy of the snail. As in most kinds of cup-shaped snails, there is no operculum. These snails cling to rocks and sometimes to the outer surface of large conchs.

The largest cup-and-saucer shells are female; the smaller ones, commonly found attached to the female's shell, are males. Should the female die or become sterile, the male grows rapidly in size and changes sex within a few weeks. The new female is capable of laying and brooding productive egg capsules.

The Imbricate Cup-and-Saucer reaches a diameter of about 1 inch and is found along the tropical shores of Central America.

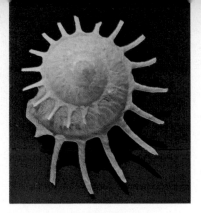

Sunburst Carrier

Stellaria solaris Linné

Once considered a great rarity, and known only from three or four specimens prior to the nineteenth century, this handsome and delicate shell has now been discovered in large numbers in the waters of the Philippines. This species lives on sandy mud bottoms at depths from 100 to 1,500 meters, but the nets of shrimp fishermen bring them to the surface.

The Sunburst Carrier was once thought to be related to the stromb conchs, but it is now known to be a distant relative of the slipper shells. The shell, including the spines, may reach a diameter of 4 inches. The numerous, perfectly formed projections around the edge of the whorls serve as a reinforcement for the otherwise delicate shell.

Japanese Carrier

Xenophora pallidula Reeve

Sometimes dubbed the "original shell collectors," the carrier shells have the curious habit of cementing foreign bodies to their shells. Some species seem to prefer to collect other dead shells, while a few seem always to attach stones or broken bits of coral. To a large extent, the selection is determined by the type of material available as the snail crawls along the bottom. In some instances, live barnacles and sponges may grow on the shell. The mass of foreign bodies probably serves as a camouflage against predatory fish.

The Japanese Carrier, growing to a diameter of 3 or 4 inches, is one of the neater collectors, although a similar species found in the Caribbean and southeast Florida is an equally good shell collector. **43**

Turk's Cup Shell

Capulus ungaricus Linné

The simple design of this common North Atlantic shell gave rise to the name, Turk's Cup, especially in western Europe where it lives in several feet of water. A few specimens have been found off eastern Canada and New England.

This inch-long shell is covered with a fuzzy outer layer, but the interior is alabaster-white. Unlike the similarly shaped true limpets, the cup shells mate and the females lay egg capsules which they brood.

Some species are parasitic and live attached to the upper valve of a scallop. A hole is bored in the bivalve's shell and the long proboscis extends into the mantle cavity of the scallop. Algal detritus inside the scallop serves as food. The males of the cup shells are considerably **44** smaller than the females.

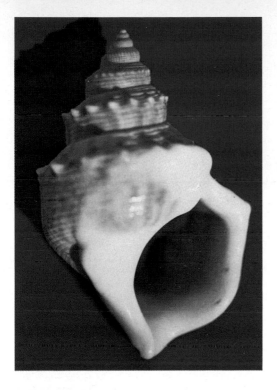

Ostrich Foot
Struthiolaria papulosa Martyn

Native to the cool waters of New Zealand and southern Australia, this group of cold-water snails was first discovered and brought back to Europe by Captain James Cook in the late 1700's.

This is the largest of the three known species, reaching a length of 3 or 4 inches. The shell is quite variable, some specimens having strong nodes on the shoulders of the last whorl, others being almost smooth. The rim of the outer lip of the shell is characteristically thick and wavy. Although the mouth of the shell is usually yellow, in some specimens it may be darkly stained with blue-black because of the dark, muddy bottom upon which some specimens live. The foot of the Ostrich Foot is small and oblong and carries a thick, brown, horny operculum. Eggs are laid by females in clumps of horny capsules. **45**

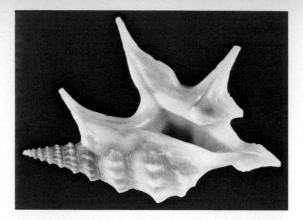

Pelican's Foot
Aporrhais pespelicani Linné

This curious little shell has been well known throughout Europe for many centuries and has delighted generations of European children because of its resemblance to a pelican's foot.

This inch-long snail is abundant off the shores of France in several feet of water. Countless thousands are brought up in the fine mesh nets of fishermen. The snail has a long, narrow operculum which it uses to polevault itself along the bottom.

There are only four or five species living today, including a long-spined, deep-water variety in southern Europe, and a 2-inch, ribbed species off the coast of New England and eastern Canada. Dozens of bizarre forms with long, curved spines have been found in the Tertiary fossil beds of Europe.

Pink Conch
Strombus gigas Linné

Of the 80 or so kinds of stromb conchs found around the world in tropical waters, none is more useful to man than the large, attractive Pink Conch of the West Indies. It is a major source of protein food in many parts of the Bahamas and is particularly delicious in salads, fritters, and chowders. Its 8- to 10-inch shell makes a favorite decoration, and in Victorian times pink and white cameos were cut from the thickest portions of the last whorl of the shell. Rarely, a moderately valuable pink **46** pearl is produced in the fleshy mantle.

Pink Conchs; below, live animal turning over by digging foot in sand

Roostertail Conch

Strombus gallus Linné

The handsome Roostertail Conch of the West Indies is considered a collector's item. Usually 6 inches in length, it is characterized by a long extension of the upper part of the outer lip. The color of the outer shell varies from a mottled chocolate-brown to a lavender or yellow hue.

They live in small colonies at depths of 20 to 40 feet, and, like other stromb conchs, they feed on delicate red or filamentous green algae. The females lay long, clear, spaghetti-like strands containing hundreds of minute eggs. Fertile eggs hatch within a few weeks.

Fighting Conch

Strombus pugilis Linné

Named many years ago because of the shell's resemblance to the spiked fist of a Roman pugilist, this docile 3-inch-long conch lives in the shallow waters of the West Indies and northeastern Brazil. Like other stromb conchs, it has a horny operculum modified into a sharp, narrow crutch with which it polevaults itself along the bottom. When annoyed by fish or crabs, the conch whips about its operculum in defense by thrashing its narrow, muscular foot.

A similar species, the Florida Fighting Conch (*S. alatus* Gmelin) is mottled with purple, has shorter spines, and is common from North Carolina to Texas.

▲ Florida Fighting Conch

▲ Roostertail Conch ▼ Fighting Conch

Violet Spider Conch
Lambis violacea Swainson

No prettier shell exists among the family of stromb conchs than this rare species from the small islands off Madagascar in the Indian Ocean. The 6-inch long Violet Spider Conch has a purple-throated shell bearing a half-dozen blades along the edge of the outer lip. During the Victorian era this was considered to be one of the rarest seashells, and even today it is difficult to obtain.

The eyes of the stromb conchs resemble colorful agates and are set at the ends of the eyestalk. Each species has a characteristic eye color, some brown with yellow circles, others blue with orange or red bands. The conchs can probably perceive the dim outline of objects.

Arthritic Spider Conch
Lambis arthritica Röding

Closely related to the true stromb conchs are the 11 species of spider conchs found only in the western Pacific and Indian Oceans. They differ in having several very long spines produced on the outer lip of the shell. However, the agate-like eyes, the foot, the operculum, and other anatomical features are identical to the true conchs.

The Arthritic Spider Conch, 5 inches long, is a common shallow-water species found only in the Indian Ocean where it lives in sandy areas covered with sparse seaweed growths. The long spines presumably prevent the snail from being readily overturned by ocean currents or predatory fish.

The Truncate Spider Conch is the largest species, reaching a length of 11 inches. Its flesh is eaten, particularly in Sri Lanka.

▲ Arthritic Spider Conch; Violet Spider Conch ▶

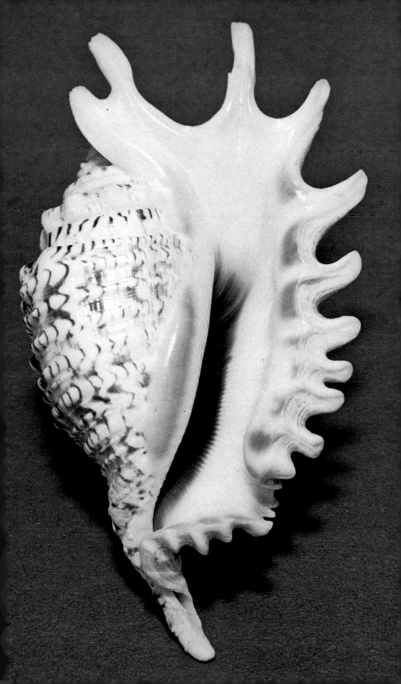

Spindle Tibia

Tibia fusus Linné

The Spindle Tibia is sufficiently uncommon and difficult to catch to be considered a collector's item. It has the longest and most delicate anterior siphonal canal of any living gastropod. Living on muddy bottoms at depths of 50 to 200 feet from southern Japan to the East Indies, the Spindle Tibia is usually buried below the surface with its long siphonal canal protruding into the water.

This species is evidently a detritus-feeder, obtaining its nutrition from decayed algae and small invertebrates. An 11-inch specimen may have a canal more than 5 inches long.

Similar, but smaller, species with shorter canals live off the coasts of India and Arabia and in the Red Sea.

Lewis' Moon Snail

Lunatia lewisi Gould

Among the most voracious of clam-eaters are the moon snails, a worldwide family of sand-dwelling univalves with large, rotund shells.

Lewis' Moon Snail reaches the size of a grapefruit and is occasionally encountered on the sand flats of the Pacific coast of the United States. It belongs to a group of moon snails that have a pliable, brown, horny operculum. The snail seeks out a large clam, envelops it in its huge, broad foot, and then bores a neat hole in the bivalve's shell. A moon snail may consume two or three clams every week. Sometimes it will attack and eat other univalves.

Similar moon snails play the same role in the ecology of the Atlantic beach areas and in eastern Asia.

Colorful Atlantic Moon

Natica canrena Linné

Members of this group of moon snails are distinguished by their hard, shelly opercula. That of the 1-inch-long Colorful Atlantic Moon is glossy white and delicately ridged. The soft foot and head of the snail are painted with red and maroon rays. When burrowing under the sand in search of clams, the moon snail uses part of its foot to cover its shell and part as a plow.

The sexes are separate in this family, and the females lay a broad, gelatinous ribbon containing hundreds of eggs. The ribbon is covered with fine sand grains as it exudes from the body of the snail and takes on the shape of a circular collar. These sandy collars are not infrequently found on intertidal sand flats. The eggs hatch in about a month.

▼ Egg collar

Tiger Cowrie

Cypraea tigris Linné

The beautiful, shiny cowries of the world's warm seas are one of the most popular families among shell collectors. There are about 200 living kinds. The highly polished appearance of the outside of the shell is produced by the soft, fleshy mantle of the snail that builds the shell. Minute, successive layers of calcium carbonate, impregnated with pigments, gradually build up the thickness of the shell.

The Tiger Cowrie, 3 to 5 inches in length, is very common in the shallow grass and dead coral areas of the Indian Ocean and the southwest Pacific. It has been sold as a souvenir to generations of travelers. **55**

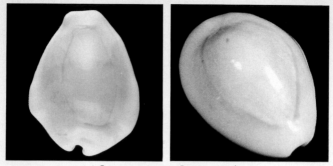

▲ *Cypraea moneta*   ▲ *Cypraea annulus*

Money Cowries

Cypraea moneta Linné
C. annulus Linné

Because of their abundance, bright coloration, and small size, the inch-long yellow cowrie and the gray, gold-ringed cowrie of the Indo-Pacific region served as a form of money for many generations. In the nineteenth century they were collected on the reef flats at low tide, cleaned in the villages, and then sacked for export to central Africa, India, and Arabia. Many tribes used them to purchase and sell slaves, to finance the building of houses, and to barter for food. Early European explorers distributed them for trading purposes among the American Indian tribes. Today these small cowries are used only in the shellcraft and shell jewelry businesses.

Atlantic Deer Cowrie

Cypraea cervus Linné

Largest of the few known cowries living in the West Indies and Florida is the brown-spotted Atlantic Deer Cowrie. Many individual shells reach a length of 4 or 5 inches, and, rarely, one may grow to 6 inches. These cowries live in sheltered areas near dead coral rock in a few feet of water.

The similar, but smaller, Zebra Cowrie is distinguished by numerous dark-brown solid spots encircled by white rings. There are only six true cowries in the western Atlantic, some ranging from Bermuda to Brazil. The Surinam cowrie lives in deep water and is most frequently captured by cutting open the stomachs of bottom-feeding fish.

▲ Atlantic Deer Cowrie ▼ Zebra Cowrie

Eyed Cowrie

Cypraea argus Linné

No cowrie demonstrates the miracle of pattern production more than the well-known, 4-inch-long Eyed Cowrie of the southwest Pacific. The fleshy mantle of each kind of cowrie produces a uniquely characteristic coloration and pattern. The shells of young cowries are thin, without shelly teeth, and usually without distinctive color patterns.

The sexes are in separate individuals. The female lays clumps of bottle-shaped capsules into which are placed hundreds of eggs. She sits protectively on top of this clutch until the young hatch out, usually in the form of microscopic, free-swimming larvae. In a few days or weeks they **58** settle to the bottom and begin to develop thicker and larger shells.

Golden Cowrie

Cypraea aurantium Gmelin

The Orange or Golden Cowrie has been greatly sought after by collectors for many centuries. Its popularity is due to its relative rarity, its beautiful, glistening orange coloration, and, because of its historical use, as a symbol of chieftainship in the Fiji Islands. The species is distributed from the Marianas Islands, south of Japan, throughout the Philippines and Solomons to Fiji.

Because the mollusk lives in sea caves at depths between 30 and 70 feet, it has not been possible to collect live ones readily until the development of scuba diving. The shell reaches a length of 4 or 5 inches and has a whitish-cream base. **59**

Leucodon Cowrie

Cypraea leucodon Broderip

In the history of shell collecting no species remained as elusive as the famous White-toothed, or Leucodon Cowrie. The first specimen was brought back to London in the early 1800's. For a hundred years no other specimen was known in collections, and many conchologists began to believe that the shell might represent a freak or possibly a hybrid. In the early 1900's a second perfect specimen was uncovered in an old collection in Boston. Finally, in 1970, a fresh specimen was found in the stomach of a huge, deep-water fish in the southern Philippines. A fourth specimen has recently been found in the Maldive Islands, south of India. All are 3½ inches long.

Prickly Helmet

Galeodea echinophora Linné

Resembling a gladiator's helmet, the Prickly Helmet of the Mediterranean is a handsome shell that was well known to the ancients. Only 3 inches in size, it sports spiral rows of small knobs and possesses a horny operculum to seal the shell aperture. Living at considerable depths on sandy bottoms, it feeds on sand dollars and other echinoderm relatives of the starfish.

Relatives of this species are abundant in the Tertiary fossil beds of Italy, but today only two kinds survive in the Mediterranean. There are two similar helmets, one living in New Zealand and the other off Japan, indicating a prehistoric connection between the world seas. **61**

Scotch Bonnet laying eggs

Scotch Bonnet

Phalium granulatum Born

Because of their pattern of squares and spiral bands, these small helmet shells were given the name of Scotch Bonnets. This common species is found in shallow water off North Carolina to the West Indies and Brazil. A very close relative is found on the Pacific side of Central America, and it is believed that they had a common origin when the Atlantic and Pacific Oceans were connected several million years ago. Throughout the world there are about 20 kinds of bonnets, most of them feeding on sand dollars and sea biscuits.

Female Scotch Bonnets, growing to the size of an orange, lay tall, circular towers of interlocking egg capsules.

Bull-mouth Helmet

Cypraecassis rufa Linné

The underside of this massive, 6-inch shell somewhat resembles the two lips of a bull, hence its popular name. The species is particularly common along the east coast of Africa where it lives in shallow, grassy areas and feeds on purple sea urchins. Adults have a very small operculum.

For centuries this beautiful shell was traded with the peoples of the Mediterranean, and specimens have been found in the ruins of ancient Pompeii in Italy. During the last three centuries the shell has been used extensively in Italy and Germany for the carving of exquisite shell cameos. It is used also as a decorative doorstop in many European homes.

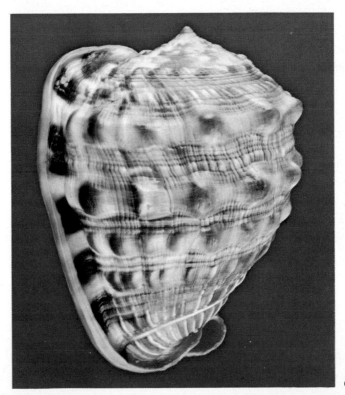

Cameo Helmet

Cassis madagascariensis Lamarck

There are fewer than a dozen kinds of true helmet shells, and they are characterized by a huge, helmet-shaped shell with a large, glossy wall bordering a toothed mouth. Largest of the helmets—reaching 10 inches in length—is the West Indian Cameo Helmet, which by curious accident received its scientific name in the belief that it came from Madagascar. This species was used to create intricate cameo scenes on a dark-brown background.

The helmet shell feeds on the long-spined sea urchin by first crushing the poisonous spines with its tough foot and then piercing the urchin's shell with its long proboscis.

Bursa Frog Shell

Bursa bufo Röding

The frog shells constitute a warm-water family of generally large shells characterized by knobbed body whorls and large, round apertures. There are two open channels, called siphonal canals, at each end of the aperture, the front one for sucking in new water over the interior gills and the back one for discharging wastes and used water.

Frog shells are usually found in pairs sheltered under coral slabs. The eggs are laid in neat, connected rows of small capsules. Frog shells are carnivorous.

Many species grow no larger than the size of a grape, but in the western Pacific there is a species large enough to be used as a trumpet by fishermen.

Winged Frog Shell ▲ Triton's Trumpet ▶

Winged Frog Shell

Ranella perca Perry

The peculiarly flattened shape of this frog shell has also inspired the name of the "maple leaf" because of its outline. The shell is abundant in certain parts of southern Japan and is used extensively in the shell jewelry business.

Although this particular 3-inch-long shell is limited to the western Pacific, there are somewhat similar shells that have a very wide distribution in West Africa, Portugal, South Africa, and in deep water off Bermuda. The reasons for these very wide occurrences are not fully understood, but one theory suggests that they are surviving remnants from ancient connecting seas.

Triton's Trumpet

Charonia tritonis Linné

Triton, the god of the sea, is customarily shown blowing a trumpet fashioned from this foot-long shell. Throughout the ages man has used this shell as a horn, but certain tribes made the "blowing hole" on the side of the shell, while others cut off the apex at the narrow end. The operculum of the triton is a large, heavy, horny trapdoor.

Triton shells feed mainly on blue *Linkia* starfish, although, in captivity, hungry specimens will feed on the famous Crown-of-thorns starfish that, in turn, eats certain species of corals.

A related triton shell lives in the Mediterranean and the West Indies.

Lotorium Frog Shell

Cymatium lotorium Linné

Many of the frog shells sport very colorful shells with reds, browns, and blacks predominating. Despite the suggestion of camouflage, the shell color has little, if any, protective value, for in nature and while alive the frog shell, which reaches 5 inches, is covered with an outer, fuzzy layer of periostracum. In some species, this epidermal-like layer consists of a heavy carpet of hair-like projections. Presumably this protective coating wards off the sponges that bore into the shell and also keeps off barnacles, oysters, and other sea creatures that might smother the frog shell with excessive growths.

There are about a hundred kinds of frog shells throughout the world.

◀ Lotorium Frog Shell
Partridge Tun ▼

Partridge Tun

Tonna perdix Linné

Best known of the 30 or so known tun shells is this one that has the color markings of a partridge. The shell is quite thin and the soft parts, including the foot, are large and tough. The proboscis of the tun is capable of enormous expansion, and two salivary glands, heavily endowed with a strong acid, can demolish a holothurian sea-cucumber with great ease. The adult tun does not possess an operculum, but the free-swimming larval form has a proportionately large one that is later shed.

The Partridge Tun, attaining a length of 5 inches, is common throughout the Indo-Pacific region.

69

Pacific Grinning Tun

Quimalea pomum Linné

One group of tun shells has produced species that have developed great, gnarled teeth in the aperture of the shell, evidently to serve as a form of protection against crab predators. These tuns do not possess a large, protective opercular trapdoor.

Only three species are found living today, the commonest being the 3-inch Pacific Grinning Tun which lives throughout the Indian and southwest Pacific Oceans. The largest Grinning Tun, reaching a size of 9 inches, comes from the Pacific shores of Central America. The third species, the Atlantic Grinning Tun, was discovered off Brazil only a few years ago.

Venus Comb Murex

Murex pecten Lightfoot

Spines are produced by many kinds of mollusks, especially among certain families of snails, such as the murex or rock shells. Champion in the production of long, delicate spines is the 6-inch-long Venus Comb Murex from the Indo-Pacific. The hard, needle-like spines are produced by extensions of the edge of the fleshy mantle. When the spines have been produced, the extensions are withdrawn from the shelly tubes and resorbed into the mantle. As the murex shell grows, former rows are bitten off by the snail in order to allow the formation of additional body whorls. The spines form a sort of cage around the snail's head which prevents fish from nibbling at the snout and fleshy tentacles.

▲ Pacific Grinning Tun; Venus Comb Murex ▶

Pink-mouthed Murex

Murex erythrostomus Swainson

The Pacific side of Central America is a haven for large, colorful murex shells that abound offshore on sand and mud bottoms where there is a plentiful supply of clams.

Of the five kinds of giant murexes, the 5-inch-long Pink-mouthed Murex is the most abundant and perhaps the most vividly painted. They are commonly brought up entangled in fishermen's nets and sold to shell shops. Rarely, the bright-pink mouth of the shell is alabaster white and denotes an albinistic condition in the shell glands.

Murex shells smother small clams in their powerful foot, and, by prying with the outer lip of the shell, force the clam to gape open. The snail then thrusts its tooth-bearing snout into the soft parts of its victim. Murex snails have a tough, horny operculum.

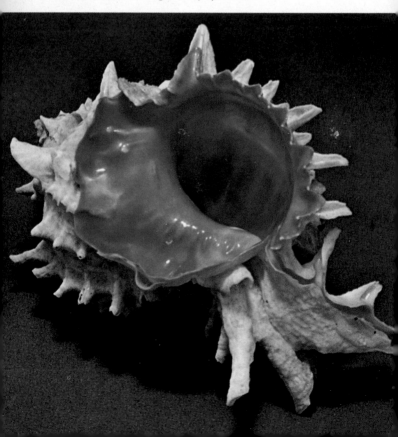

Dye Murex

Murex brandaris Linné

Thousands of years ago in the ancient world of the Mediterranean, several kinds of snails were used by the Phoenicians and Egyptians to produce the very valuable dye, Royal Tyrian Purple. The leading source was the spiny Dye Murex, a common 3-inch-long snail abundant in shallow water. The living snails were crushed in cauldrons and boiled in water for several hours. Cloth and threads dipped in this soupy bath took on a rich magenta shade. Because of the enormous number of snails required to dye a pound of cloth, the purple dye was very costly and was usually reserved for use by priests and royalty.

Most members of this mollusk family produce a dye which will cause a harmless purple stain on the fingers of shell collectors.

Rota Murex

Homalocantha anatomica Perry

In contrast to the long, delicate spines found in other rock shells, those of the Philippine Rota Murex are curved, flattened, and somewhat paddle shaped. These 2-inch snails live on the sides of large, dead coral boulders and are usually well camouflaged by heavy growths of algae, bryozoans, and sponges.

The eggs of murex shells are laid in urn-shaped capsules which the female attaches in clumps to rocks. Some species swarm together during the mating season and form a large, communal mass of capsules, sometimes the size of a basketball. Less agile participants in this rally are sometimes buried within the ball of capsules and do not escape until the young hatch and the capsules disintegrate months afterward.

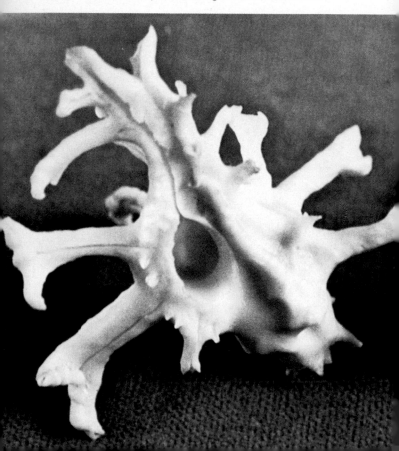

Drupe Snails
Drupa morum Röding

The small group of drupe snails belongs to the murex family, but their eight kinds are limited to the Indo-Pacific area. They are familiar members of the rocky, intertidal zone. The upper surface of the shell is usually camouflaged with sea growths, but once removed from their rock perches they reveal a very colorful underside.

Some species, such as the Morum Drupe, have a vivid purple aperture bearing a set of gnarled, shelly teeth. Other kinds, such as the Digitate Drupe, have a bright-yellow mouth.

Most drupes, all about an inch in size, feed on tiny rock barnacles and small mussels lodged in the cracks of the rock. The shell's mouth is considerably constricted with teeth, evidently to provide protection from predatory sea birds and rock crabs.

Frilled Dogwinkle

Nucella lamellosa Gmelin

Found in the cool waters all along the rocky shores of the northwest coast of America, the abundant Frilled Dogwinkle is renowned for its variability in color and sculpturing. Ranging in size from 1 to 3 inches, adults may vary in color from white to gray to orange. Sculpturing may vary from crude threads to quite thin, erect fimbriations. Their diet, consisting of barnacles, mussels, and oysters, somewhat influences the color of their shells. In rough water areas individuals may have rather smooth shells.

A gland in the mantle of the snail produces a yellowish fluid which stains cloth a vivid magenta when exposed to light and seawater.

Santa Cruz Latiaxis

Latiaxis santacruzensis Emerson and D'Attilio

Of all the delicate deep-sea snails, the Latiaxis shells exhibit the most graceful and most intricate spines. Their forms are so variable that the number of species existing in the world's oceans is not exactly known. Japanese seas harbor several dozen species.

As recently as 1970 a new species was discovered in deep water off the island of Santa Cruz, in the Galapagos Archipelago. This rare Latiaxis reaches a length of 2 inches. None of these snails has a set of radular teeth, which suggests that they suck juices from other sea creatures.

Papery Rapa

Rapa rapa Linné

A shell as lightweight and fragile as the Papery Rapa would not survive unless it lived in an unusual habitat or was protected by an unusually large and enveloping mantle. As a member of the magilid family it has a relatively small foot, head, and nonprotruding mantle. Its protection comes from its curious habit of being buried all its life in the fleshy walls of a giant soft coral. The only contact the snail has with the watery outer world is through its shelly siphonal canal. Sometimes the base of the yellow Philippine soft coral may be bored from within by dozens of these snails, which range from 1 to 3 inches in size.

New England Whelk

Neptunea lyrata decemcostata Say

This handsome, 4-inch, cold-water snail is abundant off the coast of New England where it preys on bottom-dwelling clams. The species is distributed around the northern half of North America and has several local forms, one coming from Alaska and British Columbia, another from Iceland, and one or two from off New England.

Neptune whelks have a strong, horny, brown operculum. The females lay a tower of egg capsules, usually attached to a rock or a large, dead shell. Several eggs develop within each capsule, but the larger and stronger young snails eat the smaller ones until usually only one snail survives.

The New England Whelk is one of the main foods of the cod and halibut, and it serves as an ideal fish bait. **79**

Spiral Babylon
Babylonia spirata Linné

Almost entirely limited to eastern Asia is the small group of carnivorous babylon whelks. The 2-inch-long shells are well known in the Orient where they are gathered in large numbers and sold as food in local fish markets. The shell is commonly modified into a child's whistle and sold extensively in Oriental toy shops.

The Spiral Babylon feeds on clams, and, on rare occasions when the bivalve it has devoured has been carrying shellfish poison, the snail itself will infect humans.

Except for one species in South Africa and another in India, all babylon whelks come from eastern Asia. The shells are usually ivory white, thick, and spotted with brown or orange.

Crown Conch

Melongena corona Gmelin

This attractive snail is limited to the shores of the southeast United States and east Mexico, where it abounds in large colonies on mud under the mangrove trees. Colonies are somewhat isolated and many have developed local variations in color and the number of rows of spines.

Crown Conchs feed on oysters and barnacles. They breed in early summer and the females lay a series of coin-shaped capsules into which are placed 50 to 100 eggs. The eggs hatch and pass through the larval stage within the capsule. Finally, the young perfect snails crawl out.

Adults may reach a length of 8 inches, but a subspecies on the Lower Florida Keys rarely exceeds 2 inches. A golden form occurs in southwest Florida and, rarely, an albino shell is found.

Australian Trumpet

Syrinx aruanus Linné

For many years there has been a friendly rivalry between Australian and American conchologists as to which continent possessed the largest living shelled gastropod. The debate still rages with various claims of 25 inches in length coming from both sides. Nonetheless, the Australian Trumpet is unparalleled in its rich orange color and sweeping, spiral lines.

The shell is limited to the northern shores of tropical Australia and is used by primitive natives as a boat bailer and trumpet. Originally—and erroneously—it was reported from the Aru Islands of Indonesia, hence its curious scientific name.

The young are hatched from coin-shaped capsules that are laid in close-knit rows on rocks.

▲ With egg case

Florida Horse Conch

Pleuroploca gigantea Kiener

This is the largest shelled snail living in North America and its distribution includes North Carolina southward to Florida, Texas, and east Mexico. Rarely, one finds specimens 2 feet in length.

These slow, lumbering giants feed on clams. Their egg capsules consist of numerous wafer-shaped pouches in which are placed several eggs. The young hatch as crawling snails, and during their early life they grow a beautifully colored orange shell. Later, the shell becomes dull and encrusted with barnacles and sponges.

On Sanibel Island, west Florida, there is a rare form that lacks the usual knobs on the whorls, which collectors call the "bumpless wonder of Sanibel." A similar species lives on the Pacific side of Central America.

Tulip Shell

Fasciolaria tulipa Linné

Uniquely American for the last 60 million years, the tulip shells originated in the southwestern United States. Largest of these is the 6-inch True Tulip, which has spread as far south as Brazil.

This shell lives in grassy and sandy areas where it feeds on clams. The operculum is dark brown, smooth, and very strong. The fusiform shell is cream with greenish-brown mottlings and rows of minute dots; rarely, one finds an orange-red specimen, which is apparently due to a genetic aberration. Eggs are laid in urn-shaped capsules attached to stones.

A second, smaller species, the Banded Tulip, is common from North Carolina to the Gulf of Mexico and is characterized by seven to 11 narrow, spiral lines of purple-brown. Tulip shells are commonly found in the fossil beds of central Florida.

▲ Banded Tulip laying eggs ▼ True Tulip

Distaff Spindle

Fusinus colus Linné

Spindle shells occur in the warm seas of the world and are characterized by a long siphonal canal which serves as a snorkel to obtain water when the animal is buried in sand. Spindles do not usually occur in great numbers but rather are found singly or in pairs, as seems to be the case with carnivores that feed upon sparsely distributed bivalves and sea worms. Herbivores, such as the stromb conchs, occur in large colonies in areas where there are large beds of algae.

This Distaff Spindle reaches a length of about 6 inches and is distributed throughout the Indo-Pacific Ocean where it lives in water from 6 to 60 feet in depth. The operculum is chitinous and brown and fills the round aperture of the shell.

Lightning Whelk
Busycon contrarium Conrad

The Lightning Whelk of the southeastern United States is immediately recognized by its sinistral coiling, or left-handed appearance. When held towards the viewer, with the siphonal canal down and the pearly, pointed apex up, the aperture of the shell is on the left.

The Lightning Whelk gets its name because of its axial, zigzag color streaks, but in very old, large specimens, over a foot in length, the shell becomes a solid white.

Whelks in this group lay long strings of coin-shaped capsules into which are placed dozens of eggs. The young snails, about the size of grains of rice and looking like miniature adults, crawl out of an escape hatch at the top of each capsule.

The Lightning Whelk ranges from off New Jersey to Texas.

Channeled Whelk

Busycon canaliculatum Linné

Ranging from southern Massachusetts to Florida, the common 6-inch Channeled Whelk is characterized by a squarish channel running around the spire and by a soft, velvety outer coating, or periostracum.

The *Busycon* whelks are limited to eastern North America where they constitute a nuisance in some areas because of their insatiable appetite for the hardshell clam, or quahog. The whelks dig the clams out of the sand and, with the aid of the edge of their shell, pry open the clam. In some areas of New Jersey and Maryland the whelks are gathered in large numbers, cleaned, and canned as a delicious conch meat.

The Channeled Whelk is coiled dextrally, with the aperture of the shell on the right of the viewer.

Tent Olive

Oliva porphyria Linné

The Tent Olive is the largest of this beautiful family, sometimes reaching a length of 4½ inches. The exquisite pattern on the glossy shell is never the same in any two specimens, and its resemblance to ranges of high mountains has always delighted collectors.

The Tent Olive lives in shallow to deep waters where the bottom consists of soft sand. It occurs throughout the Gulf of California to west Panama.

The beauty of the shell, produced by the mantle, is so striking that some beginning collectors mistake it for the rare and equally famous Glory-of-the-Seas Cone Shell.

There are over 60 kinds of olives throughout the world, most of them living in warm seas.

Orange-mouth Olive

Oliva sericea Röding

The Indo-Pacific region contains the most colorful of the olive shells including the 3-inch-long Orange-mouth Olive. Olives have a very long, fleshy siphonal tube which protrudes above the level of the sandy bottom. Any scent of food, such as dead fish, shrimp, or a live clam, will bring the olive to the surface. The food is covered with slime and then passed to the rear of the foot which forms a pouch for hoarding the future supply of nutrition.

After mating, the female olive lays minute, clear egg capsules about $1/10$ inch in diameter. Each capsule contains about two dozen eggs which hatch in about a week into small, free-swimming larvae.

▲ Tent Olive ▼ Orange-mouth Olive

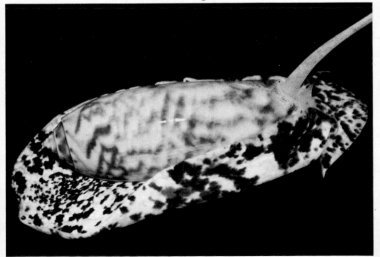

Tankerville's Ancilla

Ancilla tankervillei Swainson

Closely related to the true olive shells, the glossy *Ancilla* snails also lack an operculum. They depend upon the production of excessive, sticky mucus as a form of protection against predatory crabs and shrimp.

Tankerville's Ancilla produces a 3-inch golden-yellow shell and lives along the northeast shores of South America. Other unique kinds of marine shells are limited to this small region of the Caribbean, and it is believed that the fauna represents a living "hangover" from the Miocene period of many millions of years ago.

This beautiful shell was named in the early 1800's after the English Earl of Tankerville, a famous shell collector.

Spiny Vase
Tudicula armigera A. Adams

There are only 20 living species of vase shells, most of which are found in the Indian and Pacific Oceans. They may be recognized by the strong, squarish, spiral teeth on the inner lip, and by the spiny shoulders on the whorls. Most of these species live in the intertidal zone or in very shallow water, although a South Australian species occurs at 800 feet.

The 3-inch-long Spiny Vase lives in 10 to 120 feet of water off the northern coasts of Australia. Discovered in 1855, it was considered to be rare until rather recently, when dredging activities brought to light numerous specimens.

Most vase shells are believed to feed on clams and marine worms.

Orig. Ch. IX f. 884, 85.

Voluta Pyrum sinistrorsa.

Das linksgewundene Opferhorn. Ch.

Sp.

Zwischen Ceylon u. Coroman

del. — Kaufm. Holfort

Sacred Chank

Turbinella pyrum Linné

The most sacred of all shells is the Sacred Chank of India which has played a major role in the history of the Hindu religion. However, only "left-handed" or sinistrally coiling specimens of this 6-inch-long shell from Indian waters are revered. The Hindus relate that many years ago the god Vishnu rescued their sacred writings which had been captured and hidden in a left-handed chank. The operculum of this snail is used to make temple incense.

Only about one shell in 100,000 is left-handed, and today they command a price of many hundreds of dollars. Pictured here is one of the first specimens ever brought back to Europe. There are only two specimens in America.

West Indian Chank

Turbinella angulata Lightfoot

Largest of all the chanks is the 10-inch-long chank from the Bahamas and southern Caribbean. The handsome, heavy, golden-yellow shell is usually covered with a thick, fuzzy outer layer. The species is common in shallow water in the Bahamas and along the northern coast of Cuba, where it lives on shallow reef flats and feeds on clams and marine worms.

The females lay rows of coin-shaped capsules about the size of a fifty-cent piece. Each horny capsule contains a dozen eggs, but usually only one or two live to grow into tiny chank snails.

The three large spiral cords on the inner lip are characteristic of the chank shells.

◀ Sacred Chank ▲ West Indian Chank

Episcopal Miter
Mitra mitra Linné

The carnivorous miters make up one of the most diverse groups of tropical univalves. Several hundred species live in shallow waters in most warm parts of the world. Nocturnal in habit, they are usually buried in sand or secluded in rock crevices during the day. The proboscis of the miter snail is very long and is used to penetrate the tubes of deeply burrowing marine worms.

The Episcopal Miter, one of the largest of the family, reaches a length of 5 or 6 inches. It is characterized by the strong, spiral teeth on the inner lip and by the vivid orange spots on the outer surface of the shell. This is **94** a common shallow-water species found throughout the Indo-Pacific.

Cardinal Miter
Mitra cardinális Gmelin

Among the many colorful miters of tropical waters, the Cardinal Miter is a well-known and conspicuous member of the Pacific reef community. Usually occurring in pairs, they are most frequently found under coral slabs where they feed and lay their egg capsules. Adults reach a length of about 3 inches.

The characteristic plaits on the inner lip serve two purposes—as an additional surface for the attachment of the internal columella muscle, and as a guard against crabs and fish attempting to extract the snail.

Although a few miters live in the colder waters of the temperate zones, most live in warm tropical waters.

Florida Miter

Mitra florida Gould

Most miters of the Atlantic side of the Americas are small and dull in color, but one of the exceptions is the 2½-inch-long Florida Miter from the southeastern United States. Usually sporting an array of purplish spots on its cream-colored whorls, this relative giant is considered a collector's item. The trapdoor operculum of the miters is horny, elongate, and usually dark brown in color. Very rarely an albino specimen is found.

Recently, scuba divers have been locating this species at night along the lower Florida Keys. The seas of the Pliocene period of Florida supported many dozens of large miters, but today the family seems to be dying out.

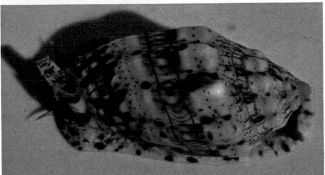

Music Volute

Voluta musica Linné

One of the most favorite families is the volute clan, consisting of several hundred large and colorful species. The typical volutes are limited to the lower Caribbean and Brazil and are among the few members of this family to have a narrow, claw-like operculum.

The well-known Music Volute, ranging in size from 2 to 3 inches, received its name because of the bars, scales, and notes ornamenting its outer whorls. The Music Volute is a member of the Caribbean region and is quite variable in coloring and in degree of development of the knobs on the shoulder of the last whorl. It is a shallow-water carnivore usually found in sandy and grassy areas.

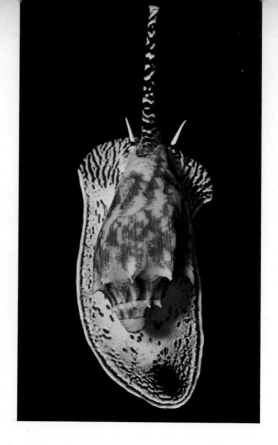

Bat Volute

Aulicina vespertilio Linné

Most common of all the volutes of the tropical seas is the 3-inch-long Bat Volute, which flourishes in the shallow waters of the Philippines and Indonesia. Each colony has its own shell characteristics, with some dark brown, others quite orange. In New Guinea, some colonies possess very heavily knobbed specimens, while in the Philippines they are commonly smooth-shouldered.

The broad, flat foot of the snail is designed for crawling rapidly over sandy bottoms. The siphon and foot are brownish gray with yellow, circular markings. There is no operculum in this group of volutes. The eggs are laid in tower-like masses of horny capsules.

Junonia

Scaphella junonia Lamarck

Limited in its distribution to the southeastern United States, the Junonia was brought back to Europe in the early 1800's and became an instant favorite of shell collectors. For years it was an expensive collector's item, and even today it is a special event when one finds a specimen washed ashore on Florida's west coast.

Attaining a length of 6 inches, the shell has purple-brown spots on its ivory-colored shell as well as on the soft parts of the animal. There is no operculum.

This species is a descendant of larger volutes that swarmed in the shallow seas that covered much of Florida during the Pliocene age, millions of years ago. The Junonia lives offshore on coarse bottoms at a water depth of 20 to 100 feet.

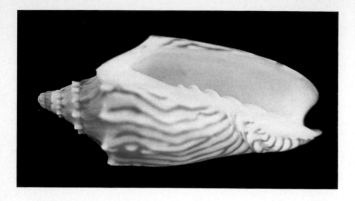

Perplicate Volute
Cymbiolacca perplicata Hedley, 1902

The Coral Sea that washes the shores of northeast Australia and New Caledonia is renowned for its unique shells, and among these is a group of small, colorful, glossy volutes belonging to the genus *Cymbiolacca*. Rarest of these, and the object of recent intensive hunting, is the Perplicate Volute, a 3-inch gem characterized by scarlet-orange, zebra-like stripes and raised plaits on the shoulder of the last whorl.

In 1973, the first live specimens were found on a coral bank in the center of the Coral Sea. The species has a red-spotted foot and lives in 30 to 100 feet of water in sandy areas near the coral reefs.

Imperial Volute
Cymbiola imperialis Lightfoot

The warm Sulu Sea between the southern Philippines and northern Borneo represents an ancient refuge for many fabulous seashells that once lived throughout the southwest Pacific. Among the largest of these survivors is the common Imperial Volute, long known to European collectors.

Adults grow to 10 inches in length. The large, teat-like early whorls at the apex are surrounded by sharp, strong, hollow spines. A rare color form lacks the dark, tent-like marks and has, instead, many narrow, zigzag, axial lines of light brown. The animal lacks an operculum.

The shell is regularly exported to other countries for the shell-
100 collecting trade.

Imperial Volute ▶

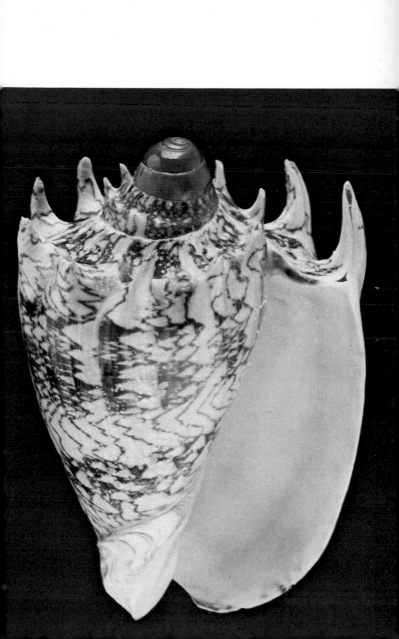

Elephant's Snout Volute

Cymbium glans Gmelin

It is appropriate that a mammoth shell resembling the snout of an elephant should come from Africa. This species has a large brown and yellow body with a broad foot. The 13-inch-long, glossy shell has a dished-out, flaring apex. Under the top layers of shell are the bulbous early whorls of the young stages of growth.

The sexes are separate in this group of volutes, and the female broods several dozen young in her oviduct. When about an inch in size, the young, shelly snails crawl out and hide in the muddy bottom. Chief among its enemies are the marauding fish that feed upon the young snails.

It is distributed along the west coast of Africa from Senegal to the Gulf of Guinea, where it is moderately common from shore to 20 feet of water.

Amoria Volute

Amoria ellioti Sowerby

There are 20 or so species of amoria volutes living on the extensive continental shelf of Australia. Evidently evolving since Australia was separated from its land connections with Asia, this beautiful group of volutes has never reached New Guinea or Indonesia.

The lustrous, smooth, and brightly colored surface is produced by a large mantle that extends over the shell. The foot of the animal is very broad and usually as brightly colored as the shell. Most species are 2 or 3 inches in size.

These species are probably carnivorous and spend much of their time gliding over the soft, sandy bottom in search of food. At low tide, when exposed to the air, they dig down under the surface.

▼Amoria Volute ▲ Elephant's Snout Volute

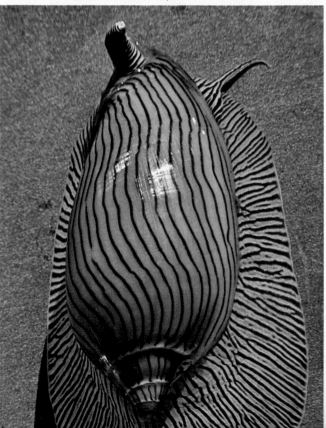

Angular Volute
Zidona dufrésnei Donovan

Unique among the volutes of South America is the 5- to 8-inch-long Angular Volute that lives at depths of 100 to 300 feet of water from Rio de Janeiro south to central Argentina.

The mantle and foot, mottled with dark green on a cream background, surround the shell and give the exterior a glossy finish. There is no operculum. The most unusual feature is the production of a long spur, sometimes an inch in length, at the apex of the shell. The shell is variable in shape and coloration, sometimes having attractive, zigzag, brown lines.

There are very few kinds of volutes in the cool waters of southern South America, and their nearest relatives live in New Zealand and southern Australia.

In this group of volutes the females produce live, shelled young.

Nutmeg Shells
Cancellaria cooperi Gabb

The nutmegs are a small and variable group of worldwide marine snails characterized by globose, well-sculptured shells bearing two or three strong plaits on the columellar lip. The animal lacks an operculum, but is able to seal its aperture from attacking crabs and bristle-worms with a mixture of mucus and sand.

The greatest concentration of species is in the Panamic Province where over two dozen kinds are found commonly from the Gulf of California to Ecuador.

The 3-inch-long Cooper's Nutmeg of California lives offshore to a depth of 1,800 feet. Seldom captured alive, it is considered a collector's item. The inner lip of the shell bears two weak, spiral cords, and the outside of the shell has numerous narrow, spiral bands of brown.

Cooper's Nutmeg ▶

▲ Costate Harp ▼ Common Pacific Harp

Harp Shells

Harpa costata Linné

There are only 14 living species of harp shells in the tropical and subtropical seas of the world. They are absent from the Caribbean. Characterized by brightly colored, strongly ribbed shells, most of them come from shallow coral waters of the Indian and southwest Pacific Oceans. They feed on small box crabs which they immobilize by smothering them in sticky mucus and sand grains.

Some species have the ability to drop off the hind end of the foot, much in the manner of some lizards trying to escape their enemies. Within a few weeks the foot is regenerated. The eggs of harp shells are laid in rows of coin-shaped capsules.

The rare Costate Harp from Mauritius in the Indian Ocean is 4 inches in length.

White-spotted Margin Shell

Marginella guttata Dillwyn

Few of the 300 kinds of margin shells are over an inch in size, but they are renowned for their glossy, jewel-like shells. Most species are tropical, with the most spectacular coming from the shallow offshore waters of West Africa. Orange-colored Caribbean species are used in making shell necklaces.

The White-spotted Margin Shell of Florida and the Caribbean is bedecked with white flecks. Most margin shells have strong plaits on the inner, columellar lip and many tiny teeth on the thickened outer lip. The animal is an active, quickly creeping carnivore, and groups of them will descend upon injured clams or other snails. The eggs are laid singly in tiny, dome-shaped capsules attached to old clam shells.

Textile Cone

Conus textile Linné

No family of marine shells has been sought after more than the cones, a group of colorful shells all having the simple and basic design of a cone. Ranging in size as adults from the half-inch Jeweled Cone of the West Indies to the gargantuan, foot-long Prometheus Cone of West Africa, the cone family contains over 400 species.

Although the shells of many species are very brightly colored, their hues are commonly hidden by natural periostracal coverings of dull brown. The Textile Cone, a 3-inch-long, common species of the Indo-Pacific, has an intricate pattern of thousands of white and yellow triangles bordered by bright-brown lines. The fleshy siphon of the textiles is painted with red, white, and blue-black.

Glory-of-the-Seas Cone

Conus gloriamaris Chemnitz

Once considered the most valuable shell in the world, this handsome and elusive cone was known only from a dozen or so examples at the turn of the century. As late as 1962 a specimen sold for $2,000, but the use of scuba gear and the discovery of several hundred specimens in the British Solomon Islands within the last few years has dethroned this queen of shells to the status of "moderately uncommon."

The first specimen, a 5-inch Philippine example, was brought back to Europe in the early 1700's. The famous English shell collector, Hugh Cuming, found three specimens under rocks on a Philippine reef in 1853, and declared that he "almost fainted with joy." There was a false report that the reef sank during an earthquake soon after Cuming's discovery.

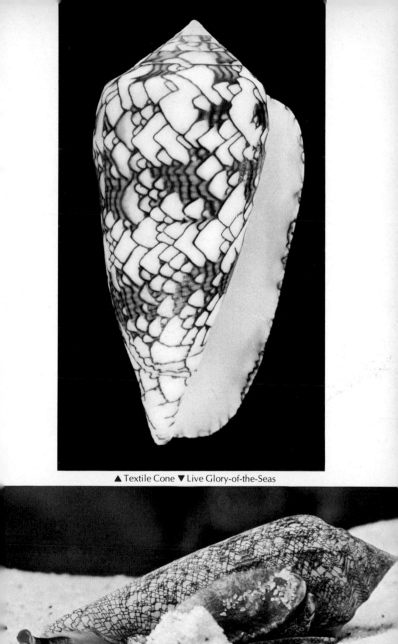

▲ Textile Cone ▼ Live Glory-of-the-Seas

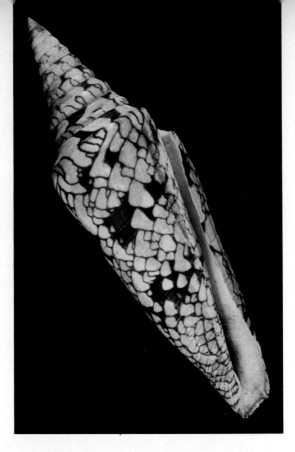

Glory-of-India Cone

Conus milneedwardsi Jousseaume

Now joining the hallowed halls of rare shells is the Glory-of-India Cone, a statuesque and strikingly patterned cone from the Indian Ocean. It was known from a single specimen brought back to France as early as 1740, but it remained unnamed, unnoticed, and of unknown provenance until the French malacologist, Jousseaume, christened it after the well-known zoologist, Milne-Edwards. Finally in the 1890's, while the first communications cable was being laid from London to Australia, five choice specimens were brought up off India, one of them 7 inches long. The latter specimen found its way into a private collection in Arabia, but its **110** whereabouts have been unknown now for over 75 years.

Geography Cone

Conus geographus Linné

At least ten human deaths have been caused by bites, or stings, from cone shells. All fatal cases have occurred in the southwest Pacific, and the majority have been due to wounds inflicted by the 4- or 5-inch-long Geography Cones.

All members of the cone family possess a poison gland in the head and have a set of minute, harpoon-shaped radular teeth that inject the neurotoxic venom into the skin of the victim. Death may occur within four or five hours if the person has been stung by a large cone shell. In some cases, shell collectors have been stung while carrying a cone in a cloth bag held against the body. Not all stings are fatal, and no serious cases have been recorded from the Americas.

Atlantic Cones

Conus regius Gmelin

Each of the major tropical oceans has its own distinctive fauna brought about by the vicissitudes of geological history, isolation, and unique ecological conditions. Second in richness to the Indo-Pacific is the Caribbean Province, which extends from Bermuda and Florida to central Brazil. Although there are probably fewer than two dozen species of cones in the western Atlantic, most of them are characterized by numerous, variable colonies.

The 2-inch Crown Cone is a common reef-dwelling species that varies tremendously in color pattern, the most unusual being a pure-yellow form. Cones are generally nocturnal in habit, and collectors must overturn coral slabs or dig in the sand to find specimens of these shy creatures.

West African Cones

Conus genuanus Linné

No part of the marine world seems more isolated and unique than the area along the northwest and central west coast of Africa. The many strange species found there show no relationships to those of Europe to the north or to those of South Africa. There is some resemblance to the species from South America, which suggests that these two great continents were adjacent to each other before they drifted apart many millions of years ago.

The Genuanus Cone, about 2 inches in length, is a colorful, glossy species characterized by spiral rows of short bars of bluish brown. It is a collector's item but not uncommon in its natural habitat of soft, muddy sand.

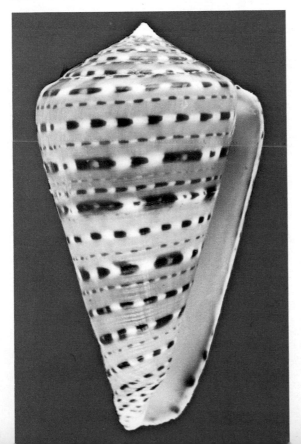

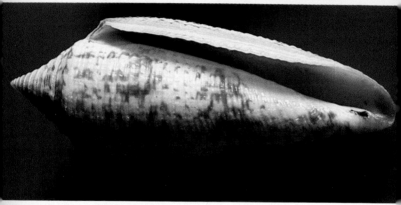

▲ Siebold Cone ▼ Austral Cone

Japanese Cones

Conus sieboldi Reeve
Conus australis Holten

Warm ocean currents, laden with food, move from southeast Asia north to bathe Japan in waters that are ideally suited to many tropical groups of mollusks. Thus, offshore in the southern parts of Japan there are many interesting and spectacular cones.

The 3-inch-long Siebold Cone, named after an early German explorer-naturalist, has a carinate spire and whorls with smooth, straight sides. In contrast, the Austral Cone has more rounded whorls and more vivid color.

Both species are moderately common in 50 to 150 feet of water and are not uncommonly brought up in shrimp-trawling nets. These cones feed on marine worms by extending their snouts down the burrows and harpooning their victims.

Panamanian Cones

Conus dalli Stearns
Conus princeps Linné

The shell fauna along the Pacific coast of Central America is very distinctive, but more closely related to that of the Caribbean than that of the Indo-Pacific. However, a few vagabonds from Polynesia have intruded in the past.

One of these is the handsome Dall's Cone, a close relative of the Textile Cone from the South Seas, believed to be a carnivore feeding on other mollusks and on worms.

Distinctly Panamanian is the Prince Cone that shows remarkable genetic variation. Although usually pastel-rose with numerous zigzag, brown axial lines, rarely, an all-golden-yellow specimen is found. In nature, this 2-inch species has a thick, fuzzy outer covering.

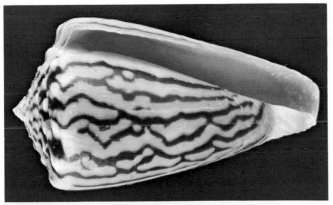

▲ Prince Cone ▼ Dall's Cone

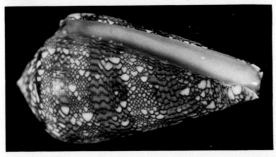

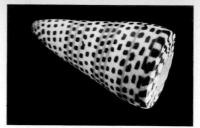

Conus litteratus

Philippine Cones

Conus litteratus Linné
Conus striatus Linné

The richest area in the world for cones is the Philippines. No complete census has been made to date, but it has been estimated that there are at least 200 species in that area.

Many of them are abundant and widespread, such as the Lettered Cone, a reef-dwelling species reaching 3 or 4 inches in size. Much rarer is the glossy Bubble Cone, 3 inches long, which is sometimes caught on hook and line by using bits of conch meat for bait.

Cones lay clusters of compressed, flask-shaped egg capsules on the underside of rocks. Some females deposit as many as a million eggs at one sitting. The free-swimming veliger stage hatches within two weeks. The young of the species that have larger and fewer eggs hatch as tiny, crawling snails.

Conus striatus

Polynesian Cones

Conus retifer Menke
Conus adamsoni Broderip

The fauna of the Polynesian islands, including the Hawaiian Archipelago, is quite sparse compared with that of the East Indies, mainly because of the lack of large, nutrient-carrying rivers. While the southwest Pacific area may have nearly 200 species of cones, there are only 45 known from Hawaii, and fewer than two dozen from Tahiti.

The Netted Cone, a 2-inch-long dweller of marine benches along coral shores, probably feeds on other small snails. The Rhododendron Cone is very rare, limited to the central Pacific, and commands a high price among shell collectors. In fresh specimens, the outside is a rich mauve and the aperture a bright yellow.

The enemies of cones include octopi, fish, small triton shells, and crabs.

Top, Netted Cone; bottom, Rhododendron Cone

Indonesian Cones

Conus victor Broderip
Conus thomae Gmelin

Because the Indonesian Archipelago stretches for nearly 3,000 miles through warm, tropical seas, it has a very rich marine fauna.

To the west it fronts the Indian Ocean and thus receives such rare species as the Victor Cone, a 3-inch, spirally striped shell. On the Pacific side, bordering the Sulu Sea, the equally unusual Thomas Cone is found in moderately shallow waters where the bottom is sandy. These two collector's items were known to European shell collectors in the early 1800's and even today are not represented in many collections.

One of the main classification features of cones is whether the spire has knobs or is entirely smooth. The operculum of most cones is very small and elongate.

Panamanian Augers

Terebra strigata Sowerby
Terebra robusta Hinds

Auger shells are worldwide tropical snails with extremely long and narrow shells. Some species may have as many as 40 whorls. A shell of equal weight, if carried upright on the snail's back, would be impossible to move, so the elongate shape has been adopted for ease in dragging the shell along the sand.

Augers are an advanced group of snails, related to the cones. Some of them have harpoon-like teeth, while others lack the radular teeth. There are about 300 living species of augers, most coming from the Indo-Pacific. The Panamanian fauna, however, stretching from the Gulf of California to Ecuador, is rich in colorful forms, such as the Zebra Auger and Robust Auger, each about 4 inches long.

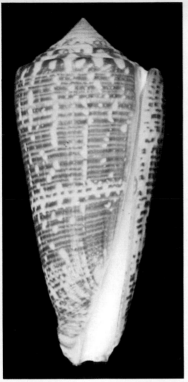

◀ Thomas Cone
▼ Victor Cone

▼ Top, Robust Auger; bottom, Zebra Auger

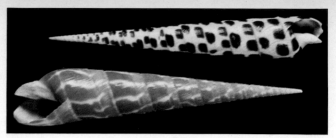

Top, Subulata Auger; bottom, Dimidiate Auger

Pacific Auger Shells

Terebra maculata Linné
Terebra subulata Linné
Terebra dimidiata Linné

The Indo-Pacific region stretching from east Africa through the East Indies to Polynesia harbors a remarkable array of auger shells, including the three common species shown here.

The heavy-shelled Marlin Spike is probably one of the largest and most common of the genus. It lives in coral sands in relatively shallow water, leaving long, winding trails. Some specimens may reach a length of 9 inches.

The Subulata Auger is a 6-inch spotted form moderately common in the southwest Pacific.

The Dimidiate Auger, marked with broad, axial streaks, has much flatter whorls. It is moderately common in the same region but usually prefers muddy sand.

The operculum in all augers is chitinous, oval, and brown.

Babylon Turrid

Lophiotoma indica Röding

This handsome, fusiform shell is moderately common in the Indian and southwest Pacific Oceans, and was brought back by early explorers. It is a member of an advanced family of snails that feed upon worms. There are over a thousand kinds of turrids of various shapes and colors, most of them living in tropical seas.

Characteristic of the turrid family is the curious slot in the upper part of the outer lip. This slot is present in order to allow waste products to be expelled easily from the mantle cavity.

The 3-inch-long Babylon Turrid lives in sandy bottoms in shallow bays. The radular teeth have been modified into short, hypodermic-like barbs in order to deliver a shot of poison to the snail's prey.

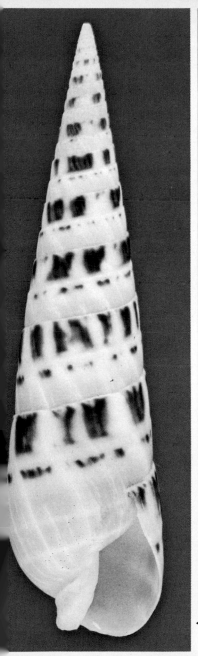

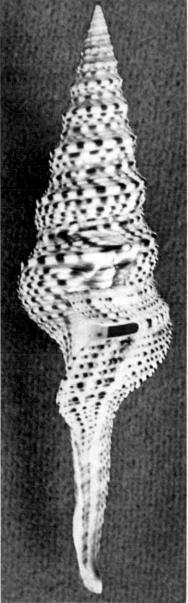

◀ Marlin Spike ▲ Babylon Turrid

Miraculous Thatcheria

Thatcheria mirabilis Sowerby

Late in the nineteenth century, this shell of beautiful design was recovered from the depths off Japan, and, since there was only one known specimen for many years, most scientists surmised that it must be a freak. But when deep-water dredging for lobsters and scallops was introduced to Japan in the 1930's, this shell reappeared. What once was a great and expensive treasure suddenly became available to the average shell collector.

The 4-inch Miraculous Thatcheria is renowned for its ramp-like, graceful spire. It belongs to a family of highly evolved, carnivorous turrid snails. This species is limited to the waters of Japan and is believed to have inspired the ancient, pagoda-like art form of that country.

Clione Snails

Clione limacina Phipps

Surprisingly, not all univalve seashells have shells. Over a thousand kinds are never born with shells, nor do they produce them as adults.

One group, the naked pteropods, consisting of about a dozen species, swarm in countless millions on the open seas. So abundant are they that some of the largest baleen whales feed almost exclusively upon them. A whale takes in an enormous gulp of water, strains it through his gigantic baleen filters, and entraps and swallows hundreds of pounds of these tiny, nutritious, swimming snails.

The distribution of these pteropods depends upon ocean currents and local temperatures. Millions of them die hourly as they drift into waters too warm or too cold for their survival, whereupon nature recycles their bodies in the depths of the ocean.

Paper Bubble

Hydatina physis Linné

In the evolution of the univalve snails there appeared a group that developed large bodies but very scant shells. The snails in this group are hermaphroditic, that is, each individual has a set of both male and female organs. Each snail is capable of producing long ribbons of thousands of eggs. When these hatch, the free-swimming larval young drift through the water to new areas and finally settle down on the bottom as miniature adults.

The bubble shells consist of several families, some with thick, globular shells, others with thin shells, such as this inch-long Paper Bubble from the Indo-Pacific and the tropical Atlantic. The snail is a moderately common species living among seaweeds in tropical bays.

Coat-of-mail Shells

Chiton species

The unique class of mollusks known as the chitons or coat-of-mail shells is represented by about 400 living species. All are less than a few inches in size, and most are rock-dwelling intertidal inhabitants.

The shelly part of these mollusks consists of eight band-like, shelly plates with a circular, leathery band, or girdle, holding these plates in place. The foot is large, broad, and muscular. The head has no eyes or tentacles; some chitons have microscopic eyes located on the upper surface of the valves. Most chitons are herbivorous, spending their nocturnal hours browsing over the algae-covered rocks. A few kinds are carnivorous and can lift their front end up and trap passing shrimp.

Most chitons range in size from 1 to 3 inches; a few are deep-sea, but most are tropical and intertidal.

Turkey Wing Ark

Arca zebra Swainson

The 3-inch-long, box-shaped Turkey Wing is a common tropical bivalve belonging to a group of families characterized by numerous, similar, small teeth along the hinge line. Covering the zebra-striped valves is a heavy, bearded outer covering, or periostracum. Typical of the ark shells is a gaping hole at the bottom of the valves. Through this the clam extends a tubular foot which spins numerous fine threads which anchor the ark to the rocks. Most of the hundred known species of arks live attached to the underledges of reefs or in sandy mud.

The Turkey Wing is used as a food in Bermuda, where it is made into a tasty, curried pie. The shells are used in the shellcraft hobby in Florida.

Bittersweet Clam

Glycymeris glycymeris Linné

This European warm-water bivalve is moderately common in shallow, sandy-bottomed bays. The bittersweet clams are a very ancient stock of clams and are an offshoot of the ark shells. The row of numerous, similar, so-called taxodont teeth in the hinge denotes a primitive condition. These clams have no well-developed siphon. Of the 70 or so species found living today, the largest is 4 inches across. Some of the bittersweet clams have strong, radial ribs, while others are quite smooth. Like most bivalves, they are edible.

The valves are proportionately very thick in this group, and the Indians of west Mexico used them extensively to fashion bracelets and amulets in the shape of sacred frogs.

127

Noble Pen Shell

Pinna nobilis Linné

The giant pen shell of the Mediterranean, reaching a length of nearly 2 feet, was well known to the ancient Greeks. Aristotle wrote about its life history and mentions a small commensal, pea-sized crab that lives in the mantle cavity of the pen shell. These rather fragile bivalves are buried deep down in the sandy bottom, and they anchor themselves firmly to underground stones by means of long, golden-colored strands of chitin. The early Mediterranean peoples learned to process these silken strands and weave a gold-like cloth.

There are about a dozen kinds of pen shells, with five living in the Atlantic. The round muscle that holds the valves together is edible and somewhat resembles sea scallop meat.

Pacific Wing Oyster

Pteria macroptera Lamarck

One great series of families of bivalves coming from tropical seas is characterized by a triangular projection of the hinge and a pearly interior. Among these are the wing oysters which have one flattish and one convex valve. The oyster produces a strong anchor of byssal threads, and, in the case of the 3-inch Pacific Wing Oyster, usually attaches itself to sea fans, or gorgonians. A relative in the southwest Pacific grows to a length of 10 inches.

The edges of the wing oysters are somewhat flexible because of the high content of water in the shell material. When the shell is collected and dried, it loses its water and splits. Rarely, this species will produce a small seed pearl.

Pearl Oyster

Pinctada margaritifera Linné

Natural pearls of gem quality come from one of half a dozen species in this group of pearl oysters. Many other bivalves and snails produce pearls, including the edible oyster and hard-shelled clam, but their finish lacks true mother-of-pearl and, hence, they are of little value.

The Pacific Pearl Oyster may grow to the size of a dinner plate and weigh four or five pounds. It lives in beds at depths of 30 to 70 feet and is attached to the bottom with strong byssal threads. Sometimes a shrimp or fish will flit into the mantle cavity for protection and, if by accident the intruder wriggles between the mantle and shell, it will be gradually entombed in layers of mother-of-pearl. In Japan, Mertens' Pearl Oyster, a much smaller species, is used to cultivate pearls.

Frons Oyster

Lopho frons Linné

A member of the edible oyster family, the Frons Oyster is only a very distant relative of the pearl oysters. It is widely distributed from Bermuda to the Gulf of Mexico and south to Brazil, where it customarily grows on the branches of sea whips. The mantle of the oyster produces shelly claspers that grow around the stems of the gorgonian. Sometimes the Frons Oyster settles on a flat stone surface or on the side of a metal buoy and, in this case, the oyster takes on a flat, circular shape.

The 1- to 2-inch oysters have so little meat inside that they are not used for food purposes, except by oyster-eating fish. The raised habitat of this oyster probably prevents attacks by starfish and avoids the chance of being smothered by drifting sands. **131**

Blue Mussel

Mytilus edulis Linné

A lover of cold water, the edible Blue Mussel is distributed around the Northern Hemisphere from Siberia and Alaska to New England and northwestern Europe. It is one of the most abundant subtidal bivalves, being found in large festoons attached to wharf pilings and rocky shores. In western Europe it is farmed on intertidal acres.

These mussels grow to a length of about 3 inches and attach themselves by means of a "beard" or clump of byssal threads. Mussels may be steamed in wine and herbs or put into seafood chowders.

In eastern Canada and the northwestern United States, Blue Mussels may, in the summer, carry an algae poison that even cooking will not destroy and that causes paralytic shellfish poisoning.

Lima File Clam

Lima scabra Born

All members of this curious family of bivalves produce numerous long tentacles along the edge of the mantle. The tentacles serve two purposes: to aid swimming and to ward off predators. A lima clam throbbing through the water is apt to attract a hungry fish, but the tentacles are very sticky and break off and entangle the mouth of the fish. Lima clams spin prodigious amounts of byssal threads which are gathered and maneuvered into protective hollow nests.

Most limas, such as this 2-inch specimen from the Caribbean and Florida, hide under protective coral-rock ledges. There are several deep-sea species whose shells reach a length of 6 inches, while a northern cold-water member rarely exceeds ½ inch. **133**

Pilgrim's Scallop

Pecten jacobaeus Linné

For centuries the Pilgrim's Scallop has been an object of design in art, sculpture, and architecture. The early Greeks imagined that the Goddess of Love, Aphrodite, was born from this shell. Much later, during the Middle Ages, this scallop became a symbol for the Christian warriors who traveled to the Near East in search of the Holy Grail. The scallop is part of the coat-of-arms of many old English families whose ancestors made pilgrimages to Spain, Italy, and Turkey.

The genus *Pecten*, whose shell may reach a diameter of 6 inches, is characterized by a cup-shaped "lower" valve and a flat "upper" valve. This and the closely related Great Scallop are used for food in Europe.

Edible Bay Scallop

Argopecten irradians Lamarck

The meat of all scallops is edible, but only those species that are large enough to be mechanically shucked find themselves in the marketplace. In the Americas, only the large, round, white muscle that holds the two valves together is eaten, but in Europe the other parts, such as the mantle and gonads, are also prepared in delicious baked dishes.

The Bay Scallop of the eastern United States lives for only two years and reaches a diameter of about 3 inches. Found from New England to Texas, it lives in shallow, protected bays among the tangles of eelgrass. The edges of the mantle are studded with dozens of bright-blue eyes that warn the scallop of approaching crabs and fish.

Lion's Paw

Lyropecten nodosus Linné

This is probably one of the most spectacular of the scallops and reaches a diameter of about 5 or 6 inches. The few radial ribs have large, water-filled nodes, and the various color phases found in different specimens may vary from a rich brick-red to scarlet, or lemon-yellow. Because it is not sufficiently common offshore from North Carolina to the Gulf of Mexico and the West Indies, this scallop does not serve as a commercial source of food. Like most large scallops, the Lion's Paw is capable of swimming by snapping shut the valves with the strong adductor muscle, thus shooting out water and producing a form of jet propulsion. By manipulating a special curtain of mantle flesh, the amount of water can be controlled at various points, thus giving the propulsion direction.

Asian Moon Scallop

Amusium pleuronectes Linné

Strangest of the scallop family is a group of deep-sea, smooth-shelled species known as the moon scallops. There are three kinds in the Pacific and two in the Atlantic, each of which reaches a diameter of about 3 or 4 inches.

Scallops are preyed upon by starfish and there are two avenues of defense: either to build a heavy shell or to develop a way to escape the starfish. The moon scallops took the latter course, and developed very light, smooth shells that can be propelled through the water with little effort. Just like the flounders that live on the sea bottom, the moon scallops have a colorful topside and a colorless bottomside, evidently a form of protective camouflage.

The Asian Moon Scallop is abundant in southeast Asia, where it occurs in large schools at depths of 50 to 120 feet. **137**

Atlantic Thorny Oyster

Spondylus americanus Hermann

Among the most magnificent bivalves is the Atlantic Thorny Oyster, which displays large, colorful spines resembling the petals of a chrysanthemum. This bivalve is really not a member of the oyster clan but a relative of the scallop.

In nature, the thorny oyster lives at a depth of about 30 to 150 feet and is normally heavily camouflaged with growths of sponges, seaweeds, and hydroids. Including spines, the shell may reach a diameter of 7 inches. Sometimes it is only possible to discern this bivalve by the gaping slit of an open specimen. All along the border of the two mantle edges are rows of tiny eyes. A passing fish or a shadow cast by a diver will cause this bivalve to snap shut.

There are about 30 species of thorny oysters found in the various seas of the world.

Giant Clam

Tridacna gigas Linné

This is the largest of the living shelled mollusks, reaching a length of about 3 feet and a weight of about 500 pounds. The giant clam lives in an upside-down position in shallow water, with its hinge resting on the bottom and with its fleshy mantle facing upward. Although it might be possible for a man's arm or foot to be caught between the flesh-bordered, gaping valves, there are no authenticated deaths due to entrapment.

Misnamed the "man-eating clam," the Giant Clam of the tropical southwest Pacific feeds mainly on algae buried in its flesh. The shell is **138** used for bird baths, punch bowls, and planters.

Giant Clam ▶

Bear Paw Clam

Hippopus hippopus Linné

Related to the Giant Tridacna Clams is the Bear Paw Clam, also limited to the tropical Indo-Pacific region. Unlike its huge relative, the *Tridacna*, the Bear Paw lacks a wide gape in the shell and does not farm as much algal food in its rather narrow mantle edge. These solitary clams grow to a length of about a foot, and the shell becomes very massive.

In the Solomon Islands, the sculpturing on the outside of the valves takes on the form of very small, curled protuberances, while in the Sulu Sea of the Philippines the shells are almost smooth. This geographical variation in morphological characters is one of the basic ingredients in the production of new species.

The Bear Paw Clam is collected in large quantities and shipped to American dealers specializing in shells.

Elegant Fimbria
Fimbria soverbii Reeve

Limited to the southwest Pacific, from southern Japan to northern Australia, the delicately sculptured Elegant Fimbria is an example of a group of clams once numerous in species and widespread during past geological times. Only two species survive today, both of which are limited to the Indo-Pacific.

The Elegant Fimbria is uncommon and grows to a length of about 3 inches. In addition to its fine, concentric ridges, it has faint, narrow, radial rays of pink on its ivory-colored valves.

Closely related are the lucines, a worldwide tropical family with strong, orbicular shells. Lacking long siphons, these clams extend a long, pencil-shaped foot through the sand, a tunnel-like substitute for the fleshy siphon found in other kinds of clams.

141

Costate Cockle

Cardium costatum Linné

The magnificent Costate Cockle of West Africa sometimes reaches the size of a grapefruit. Its handsome, sharp ribs have inspired designs in art and sculpture for many centuries.

These clams are sand-dwellers and have short siphons, hence they live near the surface and are likely to be washed out of the sand. To compensate for this, the cockles have developed a long, powerful foot that can be lashed about so quickly that the clam can jump several inches off the bottom.

Worldwide there are about 200 species of various shapes, but none with the strong ribbing of the Costate Cockle. All cockles are edible, although rather tough, and in western Europe they are extensively fished **142** and marketed.

Heart Cockle

Corculum cardissa Linné

Abundant in the southwest tropical Pacific, the curiously shaped Heart Cockle does not burrow into the soft bottom but instead lives on the surface of hard reef flats. It anchors itself by means of a strong, elastic byssus, or clump of threads.

Most of its nutrition comes from algae grown in its own flesh just under the surface of the thin shell. The broad upper surface has modified, translucent shell crystals, oriented to catch sun rays that help the algae grow.

The Heart Cockle, usually reaching 2 inches in diameter, develops a bright array of color forms, from yellow to rose, that blend in with its surroundings.

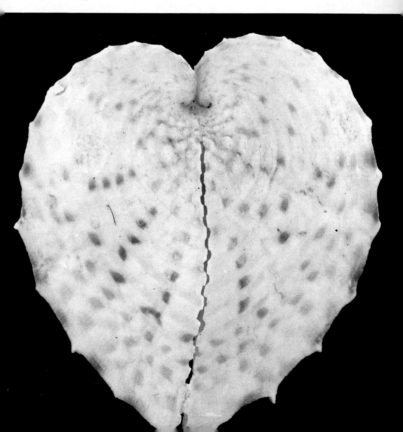

Quahog Clam

Mercenaria mercenaria Linné

The family of Venus clams is popular in most parts of the world as a source of food. These hard-shelled, sand-dwelling clams live in shallow, intertidal areas where they are easily collected by hand or with rakes. At low tide, when the sand bars are exposed, the presence of a clam can be determined by a jet of water arising from the small hole in the sand made by the clam's siphon.

Large quahogs, over 4 inches in diameter, are minced and used in chowders, but the smaller, more tender "cherrystone" individuals are served raw and chilled. The Indians of eastern North America used the shell to fashion small, bead-like pieces into wampum belts. Since only a small part of the shell is colored purple, the dark beads were more valuable than those coming from the white portions of the valves.

Wedding Cake Venus

Callanaitis disjecta Perry

The Venus clam family probably has the most species of any family. Members of this diverse group are found in all seas, and most of them are known for their attractive shells.

Australia has many unique kinds of marine shells, but one of its most unusual clams is the so-called Wedding Cake Venus, a striking 3-inch bivalve with strong, pink-colored flutings. The texture of the shell is not unlike that of a hard frosting on a wedding cake. Presumably, these shelly flutes serve as an anchor in the sand.

Venus clams stay near the surface of the sandy substrate because their siphons are very short. The foot of the Venus clam is hatchet-shaped and may be changed to the shape of an anchor by muscular contractions.

Venus Comb Clams

Venus Comb Clam

Pitar lupanarius Lesson

Long spines on clams are a rarity in nature. Among the exceptions are the thorny oysters that attach themselves to a hard substrate, and two groups of clams, one the Altamaha Mussel of Georgia rivers, the other this handsome member of the venerid clams.

The Venus Comb Clam from the eastern Pacific occurs from Baja California to Peru, while an almost identical Atlantic form lives in the West Indies. Evidently, the long, delicate spines serve as anchors to prevent intertidal waves from washing the clams out of the sand. The valves reach a length of about 2 inches, and the spines may be half that size. Minute, long, fleshy protuberances of the mantle edge secrete the tubular spines.

Golden Tellin

Tellina foliacea Linné

The fact that there are over 200 species in the tellin family indicates that these delicate, elongate clams are highly successful in a wide variety of climates and habitats. From the cold waters of Alaska to hot equatorial bays, from intertidal sand bars to depths of over six miles, the tellins have colonized the sea bottom in vast numbers. In some areas they serve as a main source of food for bottom-feeding fish.

A few species are coveted by shell collectors, and foremost among them is the handsome Golden Tellin from the southwest Pacific. This bright, orange-yellow, thin clam, reaching a length of 3 inches, lives in muddy bottoms in bays where the water is at least 50 feet in depth. It is not uncommon in the Philippines.

Sunrise Tellin

Tellina radiata Linné

One of the largest and most colorful families of bivalves is that of the tellins, a group of sand-dwelling clams with very long siphons. Most of the colorful species are found in the tropics, and the prettiest of them is the Sunrise Tellin. This common, 3-inch-long tellin is abundant in the white coral sands of the West Indies, usually at a depth of 20 to 80 feet.

Early travelers brought specimens back to Europe, and, during the shell craze of the Victorian period in England, the Sunrise Tellin was used extensively to cover the walls of shell grottoes.

The oily-smooth exterior of this species may be either creamy white or rayed with pale red. Rarely, the species is found as far north as South Carolina. In Bermuda, it is found off the south shore.

Atlantic Surf Clam

Spisula solidissima Dillwyn

More than three-quarters of all the fried and canned clams eaten in the United States are this common bivalve found in large numbers off the coast of eastern America. Although small specimens are sometimes found on the lower part of sandy beaches, the 5- to 7-inch marketable individuals live in sand in depths of water of 60 to 80 feet.

Commercial dredging boats have gradually reduced the fishery to near extinction from New York to Delaware. In previous years, a severe winter storm in New Jersey would strand over 50 million clams along a ten-mile stretch of beach.

Members of the family of surf clams are characterized by a small, spoon-shaped socket in the hinge of the valves.

▲ Gaudy Asaphis ▼

▼ Atlantic Coquina digging into sand

Gaudy Asaphis

Asaphis deflorata Linné

Although rather dull in color on its coarse exterior, the valves of the Gaudy Asaphis clam are brilliantly colored inside. There appear to be three genetically controlled color phases: a simple whitish yellow, a strongly purple-blotched, and a bright red.

The clams are intertidal, usually preferring a coarse sand interspersed with stones. The fine, coarsely beaded ribs on the exterior offer a frictional resistance to prevent the clam from being washed free by waves.

The 2- to 3-inch-long Gaudy Asaphis is common in some parts of Bermuda, Florida, and the West Indies. The meat is edible if the clams are not taken from polluted waters. The brightly colored valves are used in making floral bouquets of shells.

Wedge Clam

Donax variabilis Say

Known in various parts of the world as coquinas, wedge- or bean-clams, these small, colorful bivalves are usually found on the slopes of beaches at the point where the waves break and slide over the sand. Thousands of the inch-long clams extend their siphons for a few seconds in order to filter in food as the water temporarily covers them. As the wave retreats, the clams that were accidentally dislodged immediately dig back into the sand.

There are about 50 kinds of wedge clams throughout the warm seashores. The Atlantic Coquina, usually ½ inch in length, sports a variety of brightly colored forms. A quart of washed, live coquinas, boiled in seaweed water for 15 minutes, makes a delicious broth. The shells are used extensively in the shellcraft hobby.

Jackknife Clams

Ensis directus Conrad

Throughout the world, on sandy intertidal beaches, one is apt to find this family of clams, named because of its resemblance to a folded jackknife. Ranging when adult from 2 to 10 inches, the clam has a usually very glossy brown or speckled tan exterior. The Atlantic Jackknife Clam occurs from eastern Canada to South Carolina.

The clam lives in a deep burrow and is capable of moving up and down by means of its plunger-like foot. There are two short, separate siphons at the end facing the opening of the burrow. If dislodged from their burrows, these clams can swim very rapidly by jetting water out one end.

Jackknife Clams are tasty and are usually prepared by breading the soft parts and frying in butter.

Angel Wing

Cyrotopleura costata Linné

The snowy white and wing-like shells of this 6-inch-long clam are well known to shell collectors and tourists in Florida. In life the outer surface is covered with a natural gray layer. Holding the valves together in the area of the hinge is a chitinous pad and a shelly, butterfly-shaped cap.

The clam lives in shallow bays and usually digs into the black mud to a depth equal to three times the length of its shell. The rose-streaked siphonal ends barely protrude above the surface of the mud.

The species is common in the southeastern United States but very rare as far north as New Jersey. Rarely, the valves may be tinged with **152** pink, a condition due to environmental staining.

Angel Wing Clams; photo below shows ''spoons''

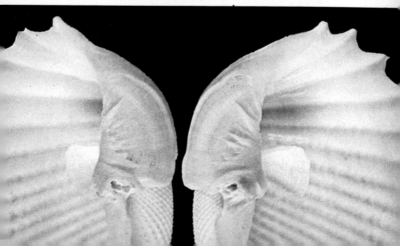

Watering Pot Clam

Penicillus australis Chenu

Probably the most unlikely-looking clam in the world is the Watering Pot, which resembles a large, shelly worm tube. Absent from the Atlantic Ocean, 6-inch-long specimens of this family of bivalves from southeast tropical Asia live buried in soft mud bottoms of shallow bays. The flaring open end bears two large, fleshy siphons that protrude out into the water. The rounded, perforated end, buried deep in the mud, represents the anterior, or front end, of this bizarre clam.

Like other bivalves, the Watering Pot begins life as a microscopic swimming larva with two shelly valves. After settling on the bottom, this species begins to bury itself very slowly, at the same time building a tunnel-like shelly tube around its siphons.

Chambered Nautilus

Nautilus pompilius Linné

The Chambered Nautilus has been known to man for many centuries and has been a part of art, craft, and poetry since the Middle Ages. Not until comparatively recently have the anatomy, biology, and habits of this relic group been known. The nautiloids roamed the seas of the world in vast numbers many millions of years ago, but today their race clings to a precarious survival in the form of only four or five species.

Now limited to the Philippines and neighboring archipelagos, the Chambered Nautilus lives in huge schools in the inky depths of about 600 to 1,200 feet. The 20 or so pearly internal chambers of the 8-inch shell are filled with water and air, thus giving the animal buoyancy. The Nautilus has about 90 arms and propels itself by jetting water through a short siphon.

Above and below, Chambered Nautilus

▲ Sectioned egg case and eggs

Paper Nautilus

Argonauta argo Linné

The argonaut, or Paper Nautilus, has been known to civilized man since earliest times, and the ancient Greeks, including Aristotle, wrote fanciful tales about this curious creature. There are about five kinds of argonauts, all of which live a pelagic life on the tropical high seas of the world.

The white, 5- to 10-inch, parchment-like "shell" is actually a temporary egg cradle built by the female of a member of the octopus family. Two of the arms of this sea-going octopus have wide, web-like flanges which, when held together, secrete the basket-shaped shell. Into this cradle are laid thousands of tiny eggs which eventually hatch into baby argonauts. The male argonauts are only one-tenth the size of the females and they do not produce a shell.

156

Index